STANDING ON THE SHOULDERS OF TITANS

SAN MARINO, LIFE AND FOOTBALL AT THE BOTTOM OF THE NATIONS LEAGUE

MAT GUY

Copyright © Mat Guy 2025
The moral rights of the author have been asserted.
Cover copyright © 1889 Books Ltd 2025

www.1889books.co.uk
ISBN: 978-1-915045-45-4

CONTENTS

Chapter One – an Announcement
Chapter Two – San Marino v Malta. June 5, 2022
Chapter Three – Malta v San Marino. June 12, 2022
Chapter Four – Latvia v Moldova. September 22, 2022
Chapter Five – Fifty-four. Minus three
Chapter Six – Islands in the Stream
Chapter Seven – San Marino v Liechtenstein. September 5, 2024
Chapter Eight – Moldova v Andorra. October 10, 2024
Chapter Nine – Liechtenstein v San Marino. November 18, 2024
Chapter Ten – Taking Stock

Chapter One – an Announcement

6 February 2024

To play this role, in this national team, you need special balls.
You need love, sacrifice, madness, passion and patience.
We must constantly takes risks and take responsibility for the cause.
It's all features I've brought into this journey, loved this shirt from start to finish.
I have defended every advantage and defect of this state with all my heart on the most beautiful and challenging fields of Europe.

With my head held high, I entered the field proud of what we represented.
With my head held high I leave this post.
Only I know the real motives behind this choice, they are many and very varied.
I know for many, being only 28 years old, this will be crazy.
I feel inside me an uncontrollable positive energy that wants to change, to explore new paths and jump head-on towards new goals.

I admit that I hardly would have found the courage to take this step a few months ago.
The climate that was in the national team would never allow me to do it, I would never leave a second family.
Now instead, I enjoy the general change.

"Be prepared to change quickly and with ever-increasing joy, there will always be someone who will shift your balance".

It's been a long journey, as long as it could have been longer.
I had fun, like a kid in an amusement park, I will never forget all the adventures, trips, retreats, and field battles with my lifetime friends.
I love each and every one of them immensely.
I would like to thank all the fans scattered around the world who have supported us crazily all these years without losing their support.

Thank you everyone.

BY AND LARGE this announcement of retirement by an international footballer could have come from anywhere. A World Cup winner perhaps. A player from one of the iconic club sides dotted about the globe, who played week-in, week-out, in the grandest, most jaw-droppingly awesome cathedrals of football known to mankind. Someone who took playing in the shadow of sheer architectural wonders – made magnificent by baying, swaying, jumping and chanting crowds of delirious support rising up into the gods far above as a matter of regular fact.

There are tell-tale signs that we read in retirement announcements all the time: the pride in wearing the shirt, in representing their country, like going to battle on the pitch for their people. A connection with the fans, fellow players – like brothers or sisters, for life, and beyond. An indescribable pride:

> *I have defended every advantage and defect of this state with all my heart on the most beautiful and challenging fields of Europe.*
> *I had fun, like a kid in an amusement park, I will never forget all the adventures, trips, retreats, and field battles with my lifetime friends.*
> *I love each and every one of them immensely.*

A pride those of us never able to achieve such a feat can only dream of, throughout life. From a young child kicking a ball in the street before dinner. A young adult – one of the swaying throng – willing on our heroes from the stands, near and far from home. An old man or woman glued to the television, a lifetime of mementos stuffed in cupboards, and memories resurfacing like firecrackers – so fresh for a second or two that it seems like we really are back there, in some foreign land, basking beneath some foreign climate – a goal long since consigned to the record books rippling the net once more. A deep breath of hot, arid, unfamiliar air, an explosion of emotion, re-ignited across time.

No matter our age, we pull on our national shirt to watch the game, and dream, of what it must feel like, to be stood, out there. We pull it on, as if it might not be too late, as if we are a part of the team. And to them, these retirees, we are:

> *I would like to thank all the fans scattered around the world who have supported us crazily all these years without losing their support.*

When it comes to national pride, *our* national team, *our* passion, *our* feeling can never be surpassed, even by those more successful. And retiring footballers, from world-beaters to also-rans, they express the same inalienable traits of pride and honour in representing their team. In facing down the very best in their region (in the above instance it is the 'beautiful and challenging fields of Europe') they become idols. Idols that we collect in football programmes, and on the back of shirts, in autograph books and photographs, newspaper cuttings in albums. Playing at the San Siro, Camp Nou, Hampden Park or Wembley.

And those halcyon days – notable victories against local rivals, against those ranked higher than you, against the greats, qualification for major tournaments, the lifting of grand trophies – no matter where your career landed, where your national team featured in the world rankings, you have something, one of the above to dine out on, to be remembered by. Surely?

We need to take a closer look at our announcement. For there are signs that we aren't dealing with your average retirement message. This one is special. Unique. Heralding the end of a special, unique international career. A career in which:

> *To play this role, in this national team, you need special balls.*
> *You need love, sacrifice, madness, passion and patience.*

A precious few have lifted the World Cup, the European Championship, but when they do, they do it in squads of 25 or so. There is a kinship, a collective.

But for this retiree, despite being a part of a team, they have also been on their own their entire career. Isolated. Prone. Taking on the world single-handed, or more accurately, gloved and with both hands. A role in which you need 'special balls', you need 'madness', along with love and passion.

Because there can only ever be one goalkeeper for the lowest ranked national football team in the world.

And after eight years and 48 international matches, this goalkeeper is retiring.

The Most Serene Republic of San Marino is a landlocked micro-state of some 23.5 square miles, encircled by the lush green of vineyards and olive groves, fruit orchards of the agricultural spine of Italy. To the east lies Rimini on the sparkling Adriatic coast, and across the beautiful Tuscan hills to the west stands Florence.

With a population of 33,000, San Marino is dwarfed in size by its city neighbours, with Rimini boasting 148,000 inhabitants, and Florence 380,000.

In the grand scheme of things this most serene republic is a speck on a map. Imperceptible on a globe.

The football-mad nation of Italy boast that their love of the game is so great, their very geography was created in the image of a footballer's leg. A boot created by the regions of Calabria, Basilicata, and Puglia taking a swing at a ball in the shape of Sicily – aiming for some unmarked Mediterranean goal between the city stanchions of Tunis on the African Peninsula and Cagliari on the island of Sardinia.

In that case, following the allegory, then San Marino would be a tiny grass stain on a football sock pulled up just beneath the knee across Tuscany and Emilia-Romagna.

Imperceptibly small it may be, but San Marino has a history as rich and unique as the national football team that represents it.

Founded as a monastic community in 301 CE by Saint Marinus – a stonemason who had helped rebuild Rimini after it had been sacked and who wanted a place to continue his devotion to early Christianity – San Marino has never been invaded, over-run, or usurped. Meaning that it is the world's oldest existing sovereign state and constitutional republic.

The capital, also called San Marino, was built by Saint Marinus on the slopes of Mount Titano, that dominates the Sammarinese skyline. In the 11th Century, the three citadel towers of Guaita, Cesta, and Montale were built, along with protective walls around the capital for an aggression that would never come. And so, the narrow-cobbled streets of San Marino remained untouched, preserved, from that day to this, where it is now a UNESCO World Heritage Site of staggering beauty.

And beneath the beauty and protection of The Three Flowers (the nickname of Guaita, Cesta, and Montale) football in San Marino was forged.

For the early part of the 20th Century football in San Marino consisted of small, local tournaments during festivities. In 1965 the Copa Titano was introduced to incorporate all the teams in the republic. Running from June to August, this annual tournament would determine the champions of San Marino, whereafter football would be mothballed in any organised state for the rest of the year.

It wasn't until 1985 that a Sammarinese league championship was introduced, running from September to May. And with that, a national team was formed.

The first ever San Marino national football team stepped out at the national stadium, Serravalle in March 1986, where they lost one-nil to the Canada Under 23 side.

In September 1987 they took part in the Mediterranean games held in Aleppo, Syria, where they played out a goalless draw with Lebanon, before losing three-nil to the hosts, and four-nil against Turkey.

In 1988 they applied and were successful in their applications to UEFA and FIFA, and in November 1990 they embarked on their journey into world football with a four-nil defeat at home to Switzerland in a European Championship qualifier.

The rest, as they say, is history. Infamy. Ridicule.

From November 1990 to March 2024 the San Marino national team played 203 competitive and friendly matches. In that time, they won just the one game – a one-nil friendly victory over fellow micro-state compatriots Liechtenstein (population 39,000) in 2004. Andy Selva, San Marino's all-time leading goal scorer with eight international goals (he also scored on three separate occasions against Belgium, and once against Austria, Bosnia and Herzegovina, Wales and Slovakia between October 1998 and October 2008) scoring the all-important and historic goal.

The other 202 fixtures have resulted in nine draws and 193 defeats. Goals scored 32. Goals against 816. That's a goal difference of -784.

In those 202 fixtures they have come up against World Cup and European Championship winners, have faced down the very best in the world. And have taken hidings in the process, the worst being a 13-0 defeat at home to Germany in 2006. (Andy Selva's second ever international goal came in a 10-1 defeat in Belgium during a World Cup Qualifier).

To say it is an uphill task for *la Serenissima* (the serene – they are also nicknamed 'The Titans' after Mount Titano) is an understatement of epic proportions. But it is a task that every player, every supporter goes into with their eyes wide open, as described by this mission statement on the National Football Association website:

> *1990 begins for the national team of the smallest republic in the world an extraordinary adventure to say the least.*
> *All of a sudden, the San Marino players, mostly amateurs, find themselves sharing the same playing field with established professionals.*
> *The technical gap is there, and it almost always collects its toll.*
> *There are extraordinary fables such as the penalty save by "Gigi" Benedettini to England captain David Platt in Wembley* (17 Feb 1993), *the draw with Turkey* (0-0 March 1993), *the lightning goal of Davide Gualtieri against England* (1-7 Sept 1993, after 8.3 seconds – at the time the fastest ever goal in World Cup qualifying history), *the victory in a friendly with Lichtenstein (*Andy Selva, San Marino's all-time record goal scorer with eight strikes across 73 international appearances scored the all-important goal in this one).
> *But mostly that of the San Marino national team is a story of David against Goliath comparisons. It is inevitable since we are talking about amateurs who see themselves as professionals.*
> *So, the concerns related to the result become secondary: The passion, the will to be there at all costs and the pride of defending ones' flag in the presence of the great European nations matters much more.*
> *Sometimes it is hard: There is no shortage of defeats in double digits. But the San Marino National Team has always looked forward, and it always will.*
> *Pride and passion do not shift with defeats, however painful they may be.*
> *The will and pride of being there, beyond the result, this is what constantly feeds the flame of those who take to the field to defend the honour of the smallest republic in the world.*

And on March 27, 2015, one Elia Benedettini took up the challenge to defend the honour of the smallest republic in the world. Pulling on his gloves, he became the goalkeeper for San Marino. Facing down Slovenia he conceded six, without reply. And so began his journey.

Elia, following in the footsteps of Uncle Gigi – who saved David Platt's penalty at Wembley in a five-nil defeat to England in February 1993 – endured, just like his uncle, tough nights against Europe's great sides.

In his 48 international matches he lost 10-0 twice, away to Croatia and home to England. He lost by nine away in Russia, eight away to Italy, and seven against Poland, Germany, and Italy (their neighbours, it would appear, do not go easy on them). Nineteen other matches ended in defeats by four goals or more.

Elia conceded 172 goals in his 48 matches – 3.5 goals per game. He did so with the Sammarinese mantra ringing in his ears:

Pride and passion do not shift with defeats, however painful they may be. The will and pride of being there, beyond the result, this is what constantly feeds the flame of those who take to the field to defend the honour of the smallest republic in the world.

Pride and passion do not shift with defeats, but they are bolstered with fables, extraordinary or otherwise – *the pride of defending ones' flag in the presence of the great European nations.*

Elia played from Astana, Kazakhstan in the far east of Europe to Windsor Park, Northern Ireland in the west. He played at the 67,000 capacity Puskas Arena in Budapest, Hungary. He played England at Wembley, Germany in Nurnberg, Italy in Cagliari and Empoli.

He faced down World Cup finals regulars in Croatia, Russia, and Denmark.

He watched from afar as San Marino scored six times during his tenure, sprinting down the pitch to celebrate. Three of those six were scored during very notable two-one defeats to Finland, Denmark, and Lithuania.

He was also a major factor in narrow two-nil defeats to the likes of Slovenia, Northern Ireland, Albania, Scotland and Belarus (12 of his 48 internationals ended two-nil). He also tended goal in three near misses in one-nil losses to Gibraltar, Moldova, and Malta.

A career many of us could only dream of, played out against some of the world's best, Elia picking the ball out of his net after strikes from the likes of Robert Lewandowski, Christian Eriksen, and Harry Kane – *I will never forget all the adventures, trips, retreats, and field battles with my lifetime friends.*

And among them, some great memories that didn't end in defeat.

In November 2020, Elia secured his first ever international clean sheet in a one-all draw with Gibraltar. A second, and last, would come nearly two years later in September 2022 with a friendly draw with the

Seychelles. In November of 2022 he would play in the Caribbean against St Lucia at the Daren Sammy Cricket ground where they would hold a team ranked 50 places higher than them in the FIFA rankings one-all.

Elia even tasted victory for San Marino in a UEFA under-21 qualifier against Wales, a victory topped off with a clean sheet in a one-nil win in 2013 against players who would go on to forge professional careers in England and Scotland.

Something that Elia himself would be called in Italy, where he played five times in Serie B for Novara Calcio.

He also played a handful of games in Serie C each for Novara Calcio and US Cesena (one of which being a Coppa Italia fixture against Lazio in the Stadio Olimpico, Rome), before 46 games in Serie D for US Pianese.

Elia's was a rich career at club and international level – life in the lower reaches of the footballing pyramid being as meaningful and packed with passion and pride as anywhere else. It is just the accolades, the trophies, the respect that is often missing. After all, you don't get to play in Serie B, more than once, you don't get to hold some of Europe's big footballing nations to defeats by just a goal or two if you don't have some ability to go with your unswerving passion and pride, your determination to represent your country with honour.

In Elia's announcement, in the Sammarinese Football Associations mission statement, we see what those lucky enough to support world-beaters see in their national team. There is no difference. Because you cannot rank national pride and identity.

And that is the magic of international football, whether you are ranked first, 50th, or 210th in the world. It is electric with belonging. Loaded with meaning. Full of joy and passion.

Life in the lower reaches of the world rankings might be tough. But that is only a small part of the story.

And even that part has been minimised further with the introduction of the UEFA Nations League.

It's first edition being played out in 2018, the UEFA Nations League was a revolutionary idea. As forward thinking as it was steeped in the time-honoured traditions of European football, it opened up a new dawn, especially for those near the foot of the world rankings.

While preserving every nation's inalienable right to be considered equal in importance and stature within UEFA, to be able to take part in World Cup and European Championship qualifiers alongside their peers – all things, and nations being equal before a ball has been kicked – the Nations League added an extra dimension.

With tradition, and respect preserved for all sides in qualifying competition, the Nations League separated teams by ability, in a league structure with four divisions: A, B, C, and D, and within those divisions, smaller groups of three or four teams. The winners of each group being promoted up into the division above, those coming last relegated down into a lower league.

And in this new structure, a new brand of football was created, especially for those nearer the foot of the pyramid. Games became far more competitive, with scorelines reflecting that. Teams that traditionally played to defend their goal, to keep the score down, became much more expansive, more expressive. (Not that life before the Nations League was all damage control. As witnessed first-hand at Hampden Park in October 2019, where a six-nil defeat did nothing to stop San Marino from breaking down the wings, swinging in crosses into the box, looking for that all-important goal).

The Nations League international window offered a consistent opportunity to play with more attacking intent. And in doing so, it helped to improve belief, confidence. Teams began to win games, sometimes regularly, where they were usually made to wait for years between victories, sometimes longer.

Nations like Kosovo, The Faroe Islands, and Luxembourg found progression, momentum, and that winning feeling that not only saw them move up out of League D but inspired their football in other ways:

Luxembourg transferred their form in the Nations League, their extra belief, into their qualifying campaigns, narrowly missing out on the 2024 European Championships in the play-offs. While club side F91 Dudelange made it through to the group stages of the Europa League twice, playing the likes of AC Milan, Olympiacos, and Sevilla in the process.

The Faroe Islands, population 55,000 built on their success in 2020, where they went unbeaten against Malta, Latvia, and Andorra in League D, going on to holding their own in League C in 2022 against Turkey, Lithuania, and Luxembourg.

And club side KÍ Klaksvik, with a squad littered with Faroese internationals became the first team from the islands to qualify for the group stages of a European competition – taking on Lille, Slovan Bratislava, and Olimpija Ljubjana in the Europa Conference League.

Kosovo, much like The Faroes, saw success translate across club football as well as international. An unbeaten Nations League campaign in 2018 against Azerbaijan, Malta, and The Faroes was followed in 2020 by a League C season against Slovenia, Greece, and Moldova where they held their own. Then, in 2022, they were pipped to the League C Group Two title by former European Championship winners Greece – finishing above Northern Ireland in the process.

At the same time, club side Ballkani qualified for the Europa Conference League group stages two seasons in a row – in 2022 playing Slavia Prague, CFR Cluj, and Sivasspor, and in 2023 against Dinamo Zagreb, Viktoria Plezň, and Astana.

Even minnow nations in Gibraltar, Liechtenstein, and Andorra found themselves winning games, drawing games, consistently. And on that basis, the Nations League can only be seen as an unqualified success in liberating teams, offering them a new way of playing, of representing their country. An unqualified success, at least, for all bar one of the countries taking part in the lower reaches of the competition.

For San Marino, in those first two Nations League seasons, they failed to make that leap. So for them, success is qualified. In both 2018 and 2020 San Marino failed to score a goal in the Nations League. As a result they didn't win in the competition either. A statistic well-documented already.

And though the Nations League may not have done what it has done for others in such a clear cut, results driven way, it has been a success through the gauze of the Sammarinese footballing mantra.

Pride and passion do not shift with defeats, however painful they may be.
The will and pride of being there, beyond the result, this is what constantly feeds the flame of those who take to the field to defend the honour of the smallest republic in the world.

Since their first Nations League fixture – a five-nil defeat to Belarus – every match has been competitive and decided by narrower margins than the die-hard San Marino supporter group, the Brigata Mai Una Gioia (Never Any Joy Brigade) were used to seeing.

By the end of that first campaign the die had been cast with close results, home and away, against Luxembourg and Moldova, and then a redemptive two-nil defeat to Belarus to round things off.

With a new-found expressiveness in being able to dictate periods of play, create chances, and threaten an all-important goal, it was this new look San Marino who took to the hallowed turf of Hampden Park a year later. And while their attacking flair did not yield a goal, it did take Scotland by surprise, their defenders expecting an easier afternoon than the one they got.

The Nations League had unlocked something in San Marino, as witnessed in the second edition in 2020, where a one-nil defeat to Gibraltar, and a two-nil loss against Liechtenstein, were followed up with two goalless draws in the return fixtures (including Elia Benedettini's first ever in international football).

San Marino's tiny population, with an even tinier pool of footballers to choose from, had closed the gap on Europe's fellow minnow nations. All that remained missing was that competitive victory…

Success is relative, and never as clear-cut as the black and white of statistics on a page – the wins and losses columns, the goals for and against – football is so much more than that.

The sense of belonging, the identity it affords us, spellbinding moments of wonder on the pitch, friendships forged off it. Places visited. Vistas enjoyed. The bustle of a foreign town in a foreign land. Celebrating who you are, where you are from, while exploring, observing how others do it. That kinship in football, crossing every barrier normally distancing us.

And that is where we are going here, via the lower reaches of the international footballing pyramid. To League D in the Nations League, exploring cultures and football rarely given much attention – unless on the receiving end of a hiding.

We have seen a glimpse with the Titans of San Marino, the lowest ranked football nation in the world, the passion, the pride of representing your country, even in seemingly perennial defeat. We have seen in Elia Benedettini the fascinating characters, with fascinating careers that inhabit these fixtures that barely create a footnote in the mainstream press.

We have learnt of the existence of the Brigata Mai Una Gioia, who devote their footballing lives to these supposed lost causes.

And now, we are going there, to see for ourselves their passion. See their love, their pride. Adventures through the overlooked footballing landscapes of Europe, with one at the very heart of it all. One at the very bottom of the pile – San Marino.

Because everyone, every football lover across the world, from Brazil to Botswana, Vietnam to Vanuatu, Spain to St Lucia, when it comes to the FIFA World Rankings, are standing on the shoulders of Titans.

But they are us. We are they. In everything but results. In victories. In success, however you define it.

It is a rich and rewarding place – League D – and we are going there now. In search of the joy of international football. Exploring the countries, the characters, and the teams that inhabit these nether regions.

And maybe, just maybe, that first ever, competitive victory for San Marino…

Chapter Two – San Marino v Malta
June 5, 2022

BORDERS ARE SO contradictory in nature. Hard lines, clearly defined on maps, swathes of land hemmed in, colour coded. They are stark, unmoving. Their existence an intimidation to those deemed unworthy of entry.

These hard lines are pure politics, meaning different things to different governments, to different political parties, pressure groups, charities, individuals. They change with the mood of the day.

Wars are fought over them. People die over them. History shows how they have changed after great conflicts. How they bulged and contracted due to colonialisation, then again after independence from such oppressions. Obsolete globes and rolled maps gathering dust in flea markets detail countries long since lost to the world. Countries remodelled, renamed. Forgotten.

But in mainland Europe, as in so many other parts of the world, on the ground, in the day to day, there are no borders.

Look the wrong way at the right moment, basking in the beautiful countryside rolling down from the Tuscan hills, and you could miss yourself leaving Italy and entering San Marino – the back of the sign indicating such a shift receding quickly in your rear-view mirror.

Look the wrong way again half an hour or so later, lost in a sea of vineyards, vines staked in rows stretching out and away from you, flashing past you with a metronomic, mesmerising quality, and you could find yourself missing San Marino altogether. Slipping back into Italy – the shimmering Adriatic Sea almost close enough to taste if not for the citrus tang of orange and lemon groves on the air – you could have unwittingly passed through an entire country without noticing. Just as neighbours, living in the day-to-day, fail to notice.

Old friends and neighbours chatting across back yards, meeting at the local café for coffee can find themselves, in the eyes of Europe's borders, on opposite sides. One from a World Cup winning country, the other from the worst footballing nation in the world.

A street, a fence, away from glory, or a footballing life with "never any joy."

Each take to their fate with a fatalistic shrug of the shoulders. Friends are still friends, neighbours are still neighbours, no matter where the border falls. With far more connecting them than separating them.

This is the way at every border – the people on each side no different in so many ways – it is just fate that has us one side or the other.

And from that side, it can often be football that helps us define what that means, to be from that side. A celebration as familiar as it is different, each celebration within each border unique – sometimes in imperceptibly small ways – and very important. A pride in belonging, even if your best friend doesn't.

A pride that can bring people together, a pride that can sometimes pit one against the other. But ultimately, a pride that everyone can understand and empathise with. And old friends from either side can still meet up over coffee, just as they have always done.

We are all not so different. And football shows us that.

San Marino, the city, population 4,000 is a prime example of San Marino, the country's way of being. It may be tiny (the fifth smallest country in the world), almost entirely lost on globes, consumed, overwhelmed by Italy on all sides, but inside its borders that bisect rolling pasture, farms and hilltops, in this 23.5 square miles, things are gloriously Sammarinese.

For example, the City of San Marino, the capital, has a population almost three times smaller than that of second city, Serravalle, where the national football stadium stands.

The city of San Marino and Serravalle are two of nine Castelli (castles). Each of these nine regions of San Marino are led by a castle captain and a castle council, and answer to the Captain's Regent – two heads of state with equal powers, elected every six months from within the coalition of political parties, ensuring everyone's voice is heard.

The City of San Marino clings to the steep slopes of Monte Titano along a series of dizzying switchbacks that wind their way up to the summit, and a scene barely changed in more than a thousand years. A UNESCO World Heritage Site, it is a labyrinth of narrow alleyways lined with rows of picturesque buildings constructed out of old, rough sandstone.

Shutters litter these homes, cafes, offices, shops, in readiness for the sun that sends a shadow slowly creeping from one side of these alleyways to the other.

The spellbound tourists wandering this ancient scene – spilling out from the cable car that drops away like a stone on its return journey down to Borgo Maggiore – all make a beeline for the battlements, the three towers.

Looking out across San Marino, Rimini, the Adriatic visible on a clear day, they all take turns peering out from their spot that teeters over the precipitous drop of Monte Titano's far side, tumbling away in a wall of rugged rock and boulder, trees somehow taken root, like lichen softening the sheer fall.

It is not quite just as Saint Marinus left it upon his death in 366 CE, but it is not far off, in look as well as attitude.

Monte Titano was gifted to Saint Marinus to enable him to create a hermitage for spiritual contemplation. And as the population slowly began to grow across the ages, the three towers of Guaita, Cesta, and Montale, along with the battlements were built from the 11th to the 14th centuries to protect from a religious or political persecution that thankfully never came.

And since the constitution of San Marino, inspired by its founder, stated that this republic would never invade, nor use war to obtain new territories, it bought land to house its growing population, that became the other eight Castelli of the nation of San Marino.

And from these foundations, modern San Marino has sprung. And exists, quietly, to this day.

It is gloriously Sammarinese that the most popular sport in the country, football, happens to be the one that they are the worst at. No great surprise given their illustrious neighbours. But what is a surprise is the source of San Marino's greatest sporting success – Baseball.

San Marino Baseball Club compete in Italy's baseball equivalent of Serie A – called Serie A.

Brought to the country in the sixties by some Sammarinese boys who had fallen in love with the game while in the U.S, they founded the club in 1970, and started life in Serie D.

By 1985 they had hit home-runs, pitched, struck-out, and fielded themselves all the way up into Serie A. Since then, they have claimed the national title of a nation that is not theirs five times, enjoying a golden spell between 2006 and 2021. They have also won the European Cup – continental Europe's baseball equivalent of the Champions League – on three occasions in 2006, 2011, and 2014.

The Stadio di Baseball di Serravalle appears as unlikely a mirage in San Marino as the baseball field from Kevin Costner's movie *Field of Dreams*. In the movie, a farmer, Ray Kinsella, builds a beautiful baseball ground among his corn fields in rural Iowa – the middle of nowhere – for the ghost of his favourite player: Shoeless Joe Jackson to play.

'If you build it, he will come', he hears as he walks through the corn.

And just like Ray Kinsella, those Sammarinese boys from the sixties did the same – bleachers behind the batting plate large enough for crowds of 1,500 to gather and idolise their own baseball heroes. The crack of ball on bat, the ripples of applause, organ music drifting across stifling, floodlit summer nights, the magic is there. Only it manifests beneath the beautiful rolling countryside of a European micro-state, not small-town USA.

And just beyond, San Marino's footballing field of dreams awaits.

San Marino Stadium is bustling expectantly. Outside, people queue to pick up tickets. A couple of young children wearing San Marino shirts so big they completely consume them, stumble on the hems as parents lead them by the hand inside.

Music plays across the PA system. A small trestle table that is the official San Marino FA shop is doing a roaring trade in scarves – a thoroughly unsuitable option for such a balmy June afternoon as this. Footballing tourists also consider the beautiful San Marino home shirt, sporting the three towers of Guaita, Cesta, and Montale from the capital that hangs in the hazy, rippling sky beyond.

And in the shadow of the main stand sporting beautiful wooden vaulted beams, the bar is doing great business in beer and hotdogs. Forty or so Malta fans who have made the trip drink and sing in the sunshine, many wearing home-made tabards like Templar Knights. The symbols of their religious order carefully stitched, drawn, painted across them being the Maltese cross, club badges from Maltese teams, images of footballing heroes old and new.

A singing, drinking, laughing, walking Bayeux tapestry of devotion to their homeland, their football history, their identity – life down among the minnows of world football does not exclude one from this. If anything, it magnifies such passion, devoid mostly of tangible, statistical successes.

But something is in the air, and beer, today, that suggests that for these travelling Maltese knights, they are in for the most rare of treats – a win, and a win away from home. And armed with that belief, their battle dress, and a good helping of beer, they take to the stands in expectation.

Taking up a position closest to the steps back down to the bar, in preparation for that all-important half-time dash, the Malta fans sing and dance, applaud, as the teams come out.

At the other end of the main stand, the Brigata Mai Una Gioia clap their heroes out onto the pitch too. Stood among their blue and white San Marino flags and banners draped across empty seats, tied to railings, this small group of 15, 20 stand with hope rather than expectation filling their hearts. After all, even in this lowly Nations League, League D clash in front of a little under 600 supporters, Malta are still 35 places higher in the FIFA rankings.

Hope. Always hope. But never any joy.

San Marino Stadium is not only the home of football in the country, but also athletics. A running track encircles the pitch, and on the far side, long jump sand pits, throwing circles, high jump mats stand in front of a small stand used to house away support when some of Europe's big hitters come to town. Today we just need the main stand.

Behind the right-hand goal more equipment for converting one sport into another lays in wait. While behind the other end, a sea of trees rise like a rich, lush, natural Kop, Curva Sud, Gallowgate End. Over its shoulder, the capital, Monte Titano looming in the haze. Indistinct. Like a dream.

It is time.

Elia Benedettini stands, arms locked around the shoulders of his teammates either side of him, beneath the hot sun.

Backs straighten, heads look up into the stand, beyond the stand, as the opening chords of 'Inno Nazionale' ring out.

A row of Sammarinese, lost for a moment, in the moment, eyes glassy, distant, focusing on a place very few of us ever reach, where the pride, meaning, belonging felt in representing your nation, lives.

A place, in the middle-distance, rippling between the heat haze – neither here nor there – a place of sacrifice. Hour upon hour, day after day, year on year of training, from a very young age, in all weather. A place of lost income from work to travel to games. A place of heavy defeats, sometime ridicule from opposing fans. A place of overcoming injury, clawing your way back to fitness, to take your place in the firing line once more. A place where everything else has to come second, in order for you to play, and come second.

We can only imagine – that place that they go. But Elia knows. It is, after all, not his first experience of this moment, shared this time with these 600 spectators.

He has experienced it many times in his international career.

He has experienced it in front of 85,000 at Wembley. He has experienced it lining up against Pirlo's Italy, twice. He has faced down the then world champions in Germany. He has travelled the continent in the name of San Marino, in the name of football.

And here he is, once more, in the slightly more humble surroundings of a Nations League Group D fixture against Malta, at that place again.

A line of proud chests, seemingly pulled up toward the sky by the music, and what it symbolises, like a row of marionettes, manipulated by the thought of those that have gone before them, those that they do it for in the present, those they hope to inspire in the future.

And as the national anthem ends, the line of Sammarinese breaks out in animation – applause, fist bumps, and hugs.

It is a moment loaded with raw emotion. The passion, meaning, and belonging. A celebration of place and people, no matter how few. No matter how small.

You can't help but feel it too. And understand that it matters. So much.

It is that understanding that has kept UEFA doggedly sticking to their belief that all nations are equal. That all nations should be afforded the same opportunity to qualify for World Cups and European Championships. That a basic respect demands this.

But also, another tournament that promotes more competitive fixtures between nations, played across international dates in the football calendar that had been traditionally used for friendlies, could only ever be a positive.

It was a moment of inspired thinking, the creation of the Nations League, having an almost immediate positive knock-on effect in performance and results of lower ranked nations.

It is rare for one institution to create such a visionary concept. Rarer even still for another to buy in to it so whole-heartedly.

It took a doubletake in the newsagents at the airport on the way out. My killing time before my flight had found me aimlessly leafing through magazines. Any magazine. It didn't matter. And there it was. A sticker album – Topps' "The Road to UEFA Nations League 2022".

Inside were blank spaces for the badges of every competing nation, the shirts of every competing nation, followed by pages showcasing goalkeepers, strikers, defenders, those with the "x-factor," playmakers, veteran players – at least two from each country. San Marino, Liechtenstein, every country.

I bought the album, as many packets of stickers as I thought I could get away with without looking completely deranged with excitement and set about discovering who had been immortalised.

As a child the Panini World Cup sticker albums had been a necessary rite of passage, collecting the stickers of the great Brazilian team of Spain '82, the Argentinians in Mexico '86. But just as captivating to me were the also rans – El Salvador, Cameroon, Kuwait, Canada. Exotic-sounding player names, wearing never before seen shirts, pictured in faraway stadiums. They held me with as much awe and wonder as Zico, Socrates, Tardelli, Maradona. Their stories, played out via cramped statistics beneath their sticker – how many times they had played for their country, the wild and wonderful names of the club sides they represented. I would wonder at what lay beyond the edges of each sticker. What the rest of the far-flung stadium in the background looked like. What their club team's shirt, badge looked like.

These early exposures fired a life-long interest in football off the beaten path. Seeing the value, the magic in places visited not nearly enough.

And here, all these years later, an album that chose to focus as much on them as anyone from the more successful nations.

Opened packet after opened packet revealed Azerbaijan's Ramil Sheydayev, Arber Zeneli of Kosovo, Noah Frick from Liechtenstein, Malta's Teddy Teuma, Vadim Rata from Moldova, Vadislavs Gutkovskis of Latvia, Kazakhstan's Baktiyar Zaynutdinov, Roy Chipolina from Gibraltar, Laifis Konstantinos of Cyprus, and one Elia Benedettini of San Marino.

A sticker album of such striking vision, a perfect companion to a football tournament aimed at benefiting all.

And as both teams broke from their huddles before kick-off to take up their formations, Elia Benedettini (sticker number 35) jogged into his goal, while Malta's Joseph Mbong (number 72) stretched his hamstrings by the centre-circle.

Adolfo Hirsch, San Marino substitute, sticker number 169, took his place on the bench. Then, when the whistle went, leant in. Looked on.

Malta may well be some 40 places better off in the FIFA World Rankings, but they are more than close enough for the Sammarinese manager to go for it. A tournament such as this, staggered through the leagues in abilities, enables even the lowliest to feel like this could be their day. And Fabrizio Constantini does.

The vocal, but small Maltese support, their tabards of flags, banners and old shirts flapping gently in the soft breeze, chant and clap, a drummer, a trumpeter leading the chorus. On such a rare occasion as being Goliath rather than David, they are here for a dominant display.

They do not get it.

San Marino are sharp, at it, snapping at every Maltese player with the ball, Michael Battistini in midfield breaking things up, setting off attacks that strikers Danilo Rinaldi and Nicola Nanni feed off, turning the visitors' back line again and again.

It is just the final ball, that decisive pass, in on goal, that fails them. But they are on top in all but that most important statistic, up on the scoreboard behind the goal.

It shouldn't be so much of a surprise, that San Marino are dictating the play, creating expansive, attacking football.

The match programme (a dying, but not yet dead institution that San Marino keep diligently at) reveals through pictures, statistics and the odd familiar-looking word or phrase San Marino's recent impressive form. At least by the standards of "the world's worst national football team."

It is amazing how many snippets you can pick up across the Germanic and Romantic languages. Familiar words that have travelled across multiple languages relatively untouched across the centuries, so as a slab of foreign text can reveal more than you'd think with a little studying. More than enough of a reason to pick up a programme – such a standard, familiar tradition – even in the Most Serene Republic of San Marino.

Through such linguistic detective work, those familiar looking words help to form a picture of a team creating a foundation to build upon.

It reveals that the only other match between Malta and San Marino ended in a narrow three-two defeat back in 2012. Striker Danilo Rinaldi's only international goal coming in that match. From his play it is clear he believes he can repeat the feat.

Another page looks back at their two friendly matches played a few months earlier. A two-one defeat to Lithuania, followed by a two-nil loss against Cape Verde. A third page reports on San Marino's first Nations League match three days earlier, and a two-nil defeat away at group favourites Estonia. A solid set of results for the Titans, given all that they must contend with.

"Davids" they may be considered, but that doesn't mean they can't play. And passion, togetherness (Elia described his team-mates as being lifetime friends), and a well-drilled set of tactics can cause problems. And they do, to the delight of the Brigata Mai Una Gioia and the majority of the 600 spectators.

Six hundred may seem paltry for an international fixture, but 600 supporters at a San Marino fixture means that roughly two percent of the entire population is in attendance. If two percent of England's residents wanted to see their national team play at the same time, Wembley would need 920,000 extra seats.

The two percent that are here are liking what they are seeing. San Marino do not dominate often, but they are doing so here. And when the Maltese coach makes two changes at the break, it does little to halt the momentum generated.

Bad fortune and psychology do that.

The second half begins as the first ended, with Sammarinese pressure and good build-up play. But that magical final element, that clinical finish on goal, remains lacking.

And when it does come, the Maltese defenders do everything they can to stop it.

Another probing run, a ball into striker Nicola Nanni, who drives into the penalty area.

A challenge.

Nanni falls.

The referee doesn't hesitate, he blows his whistle, he points to the spot.

Penalty. And a deserved chance at only a 28th Sammarinese international goal in 35 years of trying. A goal that would yield an even rarer feat – San Marino taking the lead.

The San Marino faithful find themselves drawn up out of their seats. Sitting somehow inappropriate in a moment like this. The Brigata Mai Uno Gioia tumble over the empty seats in front of them, down to the fencing at the front of the stand. As if fate, that ever-illusive joy at a goal scored is compelling them forward. Toward destiny.

They are not a raucous set of supporters. How can you be when a majority have never even seen their team win a game? They are respectful, tolerant of their louder Maltese brethren, who, for the moment, have sunk down, head in hands, drum and trumpet silenced.

But a lack of clamour, of febrile chanting does not mean a lack of care. They care about their team deeply, and want so very badly for this penalty to go in.

They cling to the fence. They cling to each other.

Down on the pitch Nicola Nanni waits as well. And waits. He was through on goal. It was his chance at glory taken away from him by desperate, last-ditch Maltese defending. It is his penalty.

Stood over the ball, lost deep in his own mind, he cuts an isolated figure amid protestations from the Maltese players, his Sammarinese brothers protecting him from the bustling and histrionics. Though it seems as if he notices nothing. None of the maelstrom around him.

Just like at the playing of the national anthems, Nicola Nanni is elsewhere. Remembering everything he had to achieve to get to this point. All that hard work and perseverance. All those long trips to the furthest corners of Europe. All those heavy defeats. And now. His chance at glory.

Nicola Nanni, like his goalkeeper Elia Benedettini, has been a journeyman among the lower reaches of Italian professional football, playing in Serie C for Monopoli, Cesena, and Lucchese. And in his four years representing his nation, he has only ever been in this position once before.

In September 2021, Nanni scored his first, and, up until this moment, only international goal, against Poland in a World Cup qualifier. That San Marino were already four-nil down by that point did nothing to dampen the euphoria. Nor did the final scoreline of seven-one.

As has been seen, victories are calculated through factors over and above the cold, hard statistics of the result here in San Marino.

The celebrations, the victory came that night in Nanni's strike being the first World Cup qualifying goal scored on home soil for eight years. Another fable for Sammarinese history books.

And now, here he is, the ball at his feet. Hopefully about to create another one.

He stares down at the ball, picturing his run up, how he is going to strike it, and where. He waits, glancing across at the referee, who has his hand to his ear.

He is listening into his earpiece, then he blows his whistle, draws a box with his fingers, and runs to a small monitor by the side of the pitch.

The curse of VAR. All the way out here. Among the beautiful rolling hills. Blighting this most wonderful field of dreams. A field that almost exclusively operates on dreams, so shorn of tangible magic created on it.

So close. So close to something special. A Nicola Nanni goal. To take the lead…

VAR. Ruins San Marino's day.

No penalty.

The players, the supporters, are crushed.

Only they truly appreciate how hard to create, and rare, these opportunities are. And it is gone, thanks to lines drawn on screens in some undisclosed location far from the longing, the yearning, cascading down from the stands, the substitutes bench, the pitch.

It is too much.

Almost immediately Malta play the ball down the field through shell-shocked Sammarinese to substitute Jan Busuttil, who hits a wicked strike from the edge of the box into the bottom corner, that Benedettini had no chance of stopping.

One-nil Malta. And a moment of joy for a player who would see almost the entirety of his international footballing career play out in 12 balmy summer days either side of this fixture.

A debut in a one-nil friendly defeat against Venezuela four days earlier would be followed by two more Nations League fixtures – his goal in Serravalle being the high-point. And that, for Jan Busuttil, would be that - bar a small cameo in a friendly against Israel three months later.

But he would always have that moment. That brilliant strike for his country.

A few minutes after Jan Busuttil's special moment, Malta have a second, final goal of the game.

What follows are a flurry of Sammarinese yellow cards, produced through a series of desperate lunges while trying to get the ball, trying to get something going, salvage something special out of a match that has slipped away from them.

The cards go a long way to manifesting, in statistics, the hurt, the disappointment felt in losing a fixture they did more than enough in to warrant some reward from.

But as well as being beautiful, football can also be cruel, unkind, maybe even unfair at times.

This is one such time, and the game ends, as so many have done before, with another notch in the loss column for San Marino.

Defeat it may be, but for Elia Benedettini, Danilo Rinaldi, Nicola Nanni and company (Adolfo Hirsch, sticker number 169 came on for the final ten minutes), and despite the disappointment of what could have been, it is still a resounding moral victory.

A moral victory with expressive, flowing play, a togetherness, a real team ethic peppered with genuine quality.

Bad result, good performance. And sometimes, when you are the smallest football nation on the continent, that has to be enough.

It seems enough for the two young children in over-size San Marino shirts, whose faces are alight with the drama and passion they just saw in their team – waving, singing as they were led away by their parents.

It seems enough for the Brigata Mai Uno Gioia, who after applauding their heroes off the pitch, set about carefully dismantling their flags and banners, packing them away in readiness for the return fixture a week later in Malta. Folding, untying with a chatter of excitement at what they had just seen, and what lies ahead.

Because there is plenty here to suggest that, in the not-too distant future, San Marino may be able to convert their results like fellow minnow nations Gibraltar, Liechtenstein, and the Faroe Islands have done. Turning good performances into wins.

Pride, endeavour, passion, they have it all in the Tuscan foothills, in this beautiful, hidden gem of a nation. And as the sun begins to set, and the shadows of San Marino's three great towers lengthen across the countryside, you can't help but want them to get that win.

When it comes, it will be more than deserved.

As the scene begins to recede, you can't help but take one last glance back in the rearview mirror before San Marino slips from sight. The floodlights of the national stadium, the bleachers of the baseball ground, the silhouette of San Marino city, suspended in the growing dusk like something from a fairytale. As you turn the corner, and it is gone, lost behind sweeping trees, as you leave its anonymous borders with some small, unseen sign, you are left with a sense that you have just left something quite special. Something rare. Something to be proud of.

And the Titans of San Marino, both on the pitch and in the stands, are just that.

On to the next match.

Pride and passion do not shift with defeats, however painful they may be. The will and pride of being there, beyond the result, this is what constantly feeds the flame of those who take to the field to defend the honour of the smallest republic in the world.

Line-ups: 05.06.22, San Marino Stadium, Serravalle

San Marino

23 Elia Benedettini
2 Allessandro D'Addario (Tommaso Zafferani 68')
3 Mirko Palazzi ©
4 Luca Ceccaroli (Fabio Tomassini 68')
5 Michele Cevoli
8 Michael Battistini (Luca Censoni 85')
9 Nicola Nanni (Marco Bernardi 85')
11 Dante Rossi
16 Danilo Rinaldi (Adolfo José Hirsch 80')
17 Alessandro Golinucci
21 Lorenzo Lunadel

Malta

1 Henry Bonello
3 Jean Borg (Zach Muscat 69')
4 Steve Borg ©
6 Matthew Guillaumier (1) (Nicolai Muscat 88')
7 Joseph Mbong (Juan Corbolan 46')
10 Jurgen Degabriele
11 Brandon Palber
13 Enrico Pepe (Fernandino Apap 90')
14 Alexander Satariano
21 Dunstan Vella (Jan Busuttil 46') (1)
23 Adam Magri Overend

Nations League D Group Two

02.06.22 – Estonia 2 San Marino 0
05.06.22 – San Marino 0 Malta 2

	P	W	D	L	F	A	Pts
Estonia	1	1	0	0	2	0	3
Malta	1	1	0	0	2	0	3
San Marino	2	0	0	2	0	4	0

Chapter Three – Malta v San Marino
June 12, 2022

THEY SAY A week is a long time in politics. In football a week is no time at all.

The strengths or weaknesses in a team cannot be lost or overcome in seven days. That sense of invincibility in a team on a roll, that dread feeling of a side shorn of confidence, sliding down the table at an alarming rate cannot be halted in one week.

The change in the psychology of a team has often been likened to making a U-turn in a tanker out at sea – a slow process, in stages through a shallow arc of progress.

What played out one week is likely, to varying degrees of certainty, to play out the next. Especially if you are playing the same team.

A national team returning home after a good away win, a home side buoyed by a progressive, attack-minded display will board the flight to the return fixture with a sense of hope, excitement at what is to come. Both psychologies having been forged by their experiences in the Nations League, where defeat isn't inevitable, where fables can be built upon to create positive results. Cold hard statistics for the plus column.

A week may well be a long time in politics, and no time at all for a manager trying to instil something new. To a man in his 50th year, but who, in truth, never really aged that much beyond his wide-eyed, football sticker crazed, nine-year-old incarnation, a week where he couldn't find anywhere selling the Topps Nations League stickers, felt like an eternity.

Days of forlornly turning through mostly empty sticker book pages, wondering which footballing minnows might belong in each spot felt like a cruelty.

Harkening back to those interminable days between receiving pocket money on a Saturday morning, walking past newsagents with boxes of Spain '82, and latterly Mexico '86 Panini sticker packets, with their brightly coloured covers promising untold treasures, the week between the San Marino – Malta matches dragged.

And just like that young boy on a Saturday morning with a 50 pence piece burning a hole in his pocket, when the day finally came to fly out to Malta, I found myself skipping through the airport terminal in the hope of finding more stickers at the news stand where I had first discovered them.

And there they were, containing the obscure gems I had been craving: Ivan Bakhar of Belarus, Jóan Símon Edmundsson from the Faroe Islands,

North Macedonia's Eljif Elmas, Sargis Adamyan from Armenia, Andorran Márcio Viera, and Khvicha Kvaratskhelia of Georgia. Welcome additions to their Kazakh, Sammarinese, Azerbaijani, Cypriot, Maltese, Moldovan, Kosovan, Gibraltarian, and Liechtensteiner brethren already collected.

In a fitting tribute to my nine-year-old former self – who no matter how carefully he tried to place the stickers within the allotted border in his album, always seemed to fix them a little askew – filling in the new stickers in my Nations League album during in-flight turbulence produced a similar outcome.

An outcome that made me smile. A beautiful, haphazard serendipity. From one captivated, awestruck little boy to another.

And this album would be kept safe, secure – a treasure for all time – just as its predecessors from Spain '82, Mexico '86 have been. With all those exotic, far-flung wonders within.

Losing myself in these stickers of footballers who never thought they would be part of an international sticker album – and maybe never would again – poring over unfamiliar shirts, badges, names, from all corners of the continent, letting my finger play across the rows of stickers (the feeling of those little indentations between new additions, each page becoming sturdier with every new sticker felt satisfying as a little boy, and still does now), I caught a shifting in the seat next to me.

A man in a suit, watching an even older man attend to his sticker collection.

His brow became furrowed. A look of mild concern growing as I concentrated while affixing each new sticker, tongue protruding slightly as I worked.

He looked at me, shifted again. Leant out into the aisle, scanning the rows for empty seats. There were none.

He sat back. Sighed. Adjusted his tie. Kept an eye on me warily.

I didn't care. I was having a wonderful time.

If San Marino is a grass stain just above the knee on the footballing leg of Italy, then Malta is a sod of turf kicked up after the boot of Calabria, Basilicata, and Apulia had struck the Sicilian ball out into the Mediterranean.

And like so many of these tiny incidentals in iconic footballing imagery – open-mouthed ballboys behind the goal, spectators risen up out of their seats by what they are seeing/about to see, defeated players looking on in despair, sprawled out on the pitch, willing for history not to be made – Malta is almost always overlooked in its part in this geographical manifestation for Italy's love of the beautiful game.

A pity, as it has a love all of its own.

Inhabited since 5,900 BCE, and home to megalithic temples dating from 3600 BCE – some of the oldest free-standing structures in the world – Malta has born witness to great empires and civilisations rising and falling.

Located just 170 miles west of Tunisia's capital Tunis, and 200 miles north of Libya's Tripoli (closer than nearly every major Italian city), with the Greek Islands to the east, it has been a melting pot of cultures, religions, and peoples for millenia.

It has been ruled by the Phoenicians, who came to prominence in 2500 BCE, then the Carthaginians, whose power grew from 814 BCE, and were succeeded by the Greeks, the Romans, great Muslim leaders, the Normans 1000 years after Christ, the Aragonese (hailing from what is now Catalan) in the 14th and 15th centuries, the Knights Hospitaller from the Crusader Kingdom of Jerusalem, who made Malta their home from 1530 – 1798.

Then came the French, followed by the British, who finally granted Malta independence in 1964, more than 4000 years after their first occupation.

As a result of such a history, it is no great surprise that Malta does things a little differently.

The tenth smallest country by area in the world – its 122 square miles sees it come in underweight to the likes of Grenada, the US Virgin Islands, and Saint Vincent and the Grenadines – it is also the only semitic-speaking country within the European Union.

Maltese, the joint official language with English on the island, comes from the same linguistic family as Arabic, Amharic (from Ethiopia), Aramaic (the language used by Jesus), Hebrew, and a host of extinct languages that passed with the falling of civilisations across the Middle East.

The capital, Valletta, with a population of just 5,000 is both the smallest capital in the entire European Union, and also the most southerly capital in Europe.

Built in the 16th century by the Knights Hospitaller, it is also one of the most beautiful.

Just like San Marino City, Valletta is a UNESCO World Heritage site. And just like its Sammarinese counterpart, is a beautiful warren of narrow alleyways lined with shuttered sandstone buildings, Baroque palaces, churches, gardens, squares, monuments, bastions and fortifications. All connected by steep pathways, that undulate like a swell rolling into the harbour beyond, across the city in large terrace steps that turn into open-air bars and hangouts once the sun goes down. Friends gathering as the shutters open, hunkering down on the steps talking, laughing over bottles of beer handed out of the windows and doors.

Small, cloistered squares – a glorious by-product of such an intricate weave of alleyways snaking between centuries old buildings adorned with vine, creeper, and gargoyles, small statues of gods, goddesses, heroic figures from ancient history perched on little plinths above cornerstones – are revolutionised as the sun slips into the shimmering mediterranean.

Houses open up. Tables are put out. Squares are converted into home-grown restaurants. Sons and daughters taking orders, pouring wine. The clunking and chinking of cutlery, utensils, frying pans. Garlic and tomatoes, fresh caught fish. Basil, oregano, all kinds of herbs and spices on the air.

A scene unchanged since those crusader knights, with their tabards sporting religious order and devotion, passed through these little scenes.

Tomorrow it would be the turn of those modern-day Maltese knights, resplendent in their lovingly stitched tabards of footballing devotion of Maltese crosses, players' faces, slogans and chants – walking, talking mini-tifos – to weave these streets, meet on the steps with friends, drink a beer or two before the big game, and the re-match with San Marino.

These steps, these squares, these gargoyles and heroes, they have seen it all, coming and going with a timelessness befitting a place like Valletta, a place like Malta.

And they will see it again tomorrow. The day after that – these places that seem to have survived time itself, the passing of history, whilst being right in the middle of it.

Not bad for a sod of turf.

Lying in bed, shutters open to catch the breeze, watching the shadows, of people passing beneath streetlamps, drifting across the ceiling, the chugging engines of boats out in the harbour, the chatter of friends on the steps below, the distant tolling of a church bell echoing across the jumble of rooftops, it was hard, right there and then, to argue against life at the foot of the Nations League.

Match day. Sunday morning. Near silence. Fragile little birds flit and cascade across a skyline littered with domes, towers and spires, scavenging patches of lichen lodged among crumbling stonework for bugs and insects. A cat looks warily on as the odd soul sweeps the steps outside their doors. Slow, measured strokes completed more out of tradition than necessity, the pop-up bars long since receded leaving little trace of their being there.

Valletta protrudes out into the shimmering Mediterranean like an ancient promenade. Surrounded by water already too bright to look at, the hot summer sun, even at this time, glistening and glinting on the glassy dead calm, laughter from across the harbour, from Birgu waterfront, Fort Rinella, drifts on what little breeze there is.

Elsewhere, as you walk the streets, the snapping of shutters folding back on themselves, the rich smell of coffee wafting. The beautiful, haunting strains of worship in song, the chiming of bells emanating from a long, thin, ornately decorated wooden door, set within an even larger wooden façade. Shadowy figures barely visible within, a barefoot woman in a brightly coloured dress, head and shoulders covered in a white shawl, leans against the opening, looking in. Captured by the scene, as I have been.

I have no idea what religion it might be, what denomination of that religion it is. In the melting pot that is Malta, awash with influence from all corners of the region, it could be anything. There are no signs, other than it is Sunday morning. And it is lyrical, lilting, mesmerising. That is enough.

Elsewhere, in little alcoves accessed by narrow, sheer pathways down, ramshackle beach huts have been constructed, teetering into the harbour on the little land afforded them. Brightly painted sandstone lean-to's, they prop each other up in terraces over the rock beach that slips down into the sea. Murals of fishing boats have been painted on walls, a little café selling fizzy pop and snacks sets up plastic chairs outside while families begin to settle in for the day.

Along one little pathway through a huddle of stone huts, even smaller, cat-sized huts, all as brightly painted as those afforded the humans shows signs of activity. The cats living in them stirring, sunbathing, readying themselves for what is clearly a daily ritual of the owner of the cafe bringing across scraps of fish, meat, whatever, leftover from sandwich preparation.

Above, on one of the fortifications that have been converted into lush green parks with welcome shade beneath poplar trees, a wedding ceremony is being readied. Next to the park's entrance a display commemorating the bravery of the island during the siege of Malta in World War II.

For two and a half years, between June 1940 and November 1942, Malta was laid siege by Fascist Italy and Nazi Germany, in the hope of breaking the allies war effort in North Africa and pushing them out of the Mediterranean.

For two and a half years Malta was bombed by sea and air, protected as best it could be by the RAF and the Royal Navy. For two and a half years it held out beneath more than 3,000 bombing raids – it is a wonder that the beauty of Valletta remains – and thanks to the fortitude of the Maltese the siege was thwarted, the battle for North Africa won, and the tide of the war was turned.

It is well that the Maltese have a siege mentality built within them. It has held them in good stead for a bruising life in international football.

The first ever Maltese National team took to the pitch in 1957, playing out a three-two defeat against Austria.

Joining FIFA two years later, and then UEFA in 1960, they embarked on their first European Championship qualifying campaign in 1962, and their first World Cup qualifiers in 1971.

Progress for such a small nation was predictably slow.

It took Malta 13 years to chalk up their first competitive victory, a two-nil win over Greece in 1975. It would take another seven for their second (two-one against Iceland in 1982), and a further 11 years for their third win, and their first away from home with a one-nil victory against Estonia in 1993.

And like San Marino, among the statistics, fables were created – good and bad.

In 1983 they suffered their heaviest ever defeat, losing 12-1 to Spain. But then, a year later they held eventual World Cup '86 runners-up West Germany to just a three-two win. And in 2008 they felt what it was like to be thumper, not the thumped with a seven-one friendly win over Liechtenstein.

But in competitive football, and 233 World Cup and European Championship qualifiers between 1962 and 2022, Malta have won just seven, drawn 26, and lost 199. In that time, they have scored 96. But conceded 665.

An unenviable record.

Unless you are Sammarinese.

But like San Marino, Liechtenstein, Andorra, Gibraltar and the rest of the perennial European minnow footballing nations, the Nations League has offered something new.

Just like San Marino, Malta made a slow start to life in this new competition. The 2018 edition seeing them lose five-nil to Kosovo at home, followed by three-one away losses to the Faroe Islands and Kosovo again. But two draws with Azerbaijan and a one-all draw at home to the Faroes in the final match gave them something to build on. And build on it they did.

Once more a slow start saw Malta lose 3-2 in Torshavn, capital of the Faroe Islands, in their opening game of the 2020 Nations League D, group one campaign.

Draws at home to Latvia and away to Andorra followed, before a formative moment that seemed to ignite Malta's belief in the Nations League.

Steve Borg's goal in the 97th minute in Riga gave Malta a first ever Nations league win, that was followed up by a second, and a three-one home defeat of Andorra.

In the last game of the group – to determine who would finish top and gain promotion into League C – there was redemption for Matthew Guillaumier, who had scored an own goal against Latvia earlier in the campaign to deny Malta victory.

With a goal in the 54th minute, he set his side up with a shot at League D glory. And it was only a goal towards the end of the game by Faroese left back Ari Jónsson that denied them.

But nine points won, only one defeat, and a positive goal difference had a revitalising effect on the Maltese national team. And barring a four-day glitch in November 2021 where they lost seven-one to Croatia on the 11th, followed by a six-nil loss to Slovakia on the 14th, confidence and belief built in the Nations League has had a positive effect on World Cup and Euro's qualifiers.

They may not have translated into a slew of victories, but that Nations League base was built upon in World Cup qualifiers (11th – 14th November 2021 excepting) with narrow losses to Russia, Croatia, and Slovenia, an impressive two-all draw in Slovakia, and four points gained over Cyprus (three-nil at home, two-all away).

And now, with the 2022 Nations League upon them, and a win under their belt in their first match, spirits were high.

But while a week may not be a long time in football, it can certainly be long enough to prove chastening, tough to stomach, and heart-breaking.

Four days after their victory in Serravalle, Malta suffered a two-one defeat to Estonia at Ta' Qali, the national stadium of Malta.

A 94th minute sucker punch by former Motherwell, Dundee United and Hibs striker Henry Anier – who had to swap the sweltering chaos of the Thai League One, and a stint at Muangthong United for this Nations League international window – had done much to dampen the positive mood around Maltese football.

Worse was to come.

The following day, news broke that Mark Piscopo, national team kit man, had passed away.

With a 12-year stint as kit man, 52-year-old Piscopo, or "Il-Lullu" as he was better known, had laid out kit, cracked jokes, been a shoulder to cry on, and a source of encouragement and friendship after heavy defeats on 104 occasions, dating back to a first match against Israel in Tel Aviv in 2010.

Described as the unseen heart and soul of the national team – a man without the skills on the pitch to represent his nation – he found a way off it to be of service, to get as close as he could to that life he so loved.

Stepping up from kit man at Floriana, his boyhood club, to the national team, "Il-Lullu's" passion and dedication, his sacrifice, humility, and friendship, his all-out love for his national team epitomises just how important teams like Malta really are.

No matter that they are down among League D, they instil such passion, create such meaning, a sense of belonging and identity. Crystalised for a moment in time in the passing of someone who embodied it all. Who had become close friends, a confidante with those who he saw as heroes, idols. Who put on that red kit with the Maltese cross, that had been laid out so carefully, with such love and respect, awe, 104 times.

Whose bear hugs and warms smiles, words of encouragement, the pride and love for those privileged enough to pull those shirts over their heads radiating out across changing rooms from Kazakhstan to Iceland, it would all be sorely missed.

The hush of Mdina, "The Silent City," seemed an apt place to be to mark the passing of such a spiritual brother, a kindred spirit in football down among the teams of League D.

Dating back to the 8th Century BCE when a Phoenician colony named it Ann, their island capital, it was then taken over by the Romans, who called this walled city Melita.

After a period of Byzantine rule, it was left abandoned and uninhabited until the 11th Century when it was renamed as Madīnah and made the Maltese capital once more. But in 1530 it was passed over again, its population dwindled as its importance faded, and Mdina slipped from a city to a relic.

Beyond the vast, imposing city walls a hush descends. The bustle of Rabat, a town that has grown out toward Mdina's grand façade, slipping away to nothing. Silence.

Labyrinthine alleyways, barely wide enough for two people to walk shoulder to shoulder, weave between grand sandstone buildings that glow a brilliant ochre beneath the hot morning sun.

Turn after turn is taken into similarly empty passages cowering beneath vast, looming walls of sandstone, occasionally interrupted by the odd shutter, a little wooden door that look as if they haven't been opened in centuries. Just the odd tourist wandering slack-jawed at the timelessness, the silence of something so grand, so imposing, that was once so important, interrupts Mdina's hush.

Where the bustle of Valletta, the vibrant clash of locals and visitors busying themselves makes it hard to feel the ghosts of a place older than history, in Mdina it is overwhelming. Thousands of years, across empires and civilisations, long-dead languages, war, siege – in Mdina the ghosts of Malta rule, and the vastness of time is tangible.

The countless Mark Piscopos, who have woven the fabric of Malta. Who have loved, sacrificed, contributed to the physical, spiritual, and cultural DNA of this small island nation. In Mdina it is quiet enough for you to see them. To feel them. It is humbling.

Befitting a country with so much of it, the history of football in Malta goes back much further than the national team.

While international football didn't materialise in earnest until the 1960's, there has been a Maltese football league since 1909, and many of its participants have been there from the early years.

"Il-Lullu's" beloved Floriana and Sliema Wanderers have been ever present, while Valletta and Ħamrun Spartans joined in 1911.

Between these four elder statesmen, the league title has been won 87 times, with Sliema Wanderers having a slightly better record of success than the others, with 26 wins, 31 runners-up spots, and 19 third place finishes to their name.

On the bus back from Mdina to Valletta, as we start to traverse through the conurbations and suburbs that fan out from the shores of the grand harbour, fan shops/bars begin to litter the cluttered streets. First a Ħamrun Spartans shop – shuttered and dark on a Sunday morning – but decorated with flags sporting the red and black, the spartan helmet on their club badge. Banners limp in the still, balmy air.

Further on and a shop adorned in the green and white of Floriana. Little units of devotion, a place to congregate, these like-minded souls, who don't have the luxury of a football stadium to call home.

Indeed, only one set of Maltese fans do, that of Hibernians. Though, ironically, the Hibs play most of their games, along with the rest of the league, at the national stadium and the smaller Centenary Stadium nearby.

With a wonderful, glorious, baffling eccentricity that is the preserve of footballing institutions the world over, the 3,000 capacity Tony Bezzina Stadium is mostly only used for first team training and Maltese second tier matches on the weekends. Competitive Hibernians matches there have been limited to fixtures in the opening rounds European qualifying – starting with a two-one defeat to Uralmash Yekaterinburg in the Intertoto Cup in 1996.

As the bus wound its way, a flash of colour in the dappled courtyard of a hotel made me sit up. Beneath the shade of a canopy of trees, the track-suited players of the San Marino national team had assembled. Some sat about tables drinking coffee, others wandered, lost in thought around the hotel grounds. Killing time. Those interminable hours before kick-off.

A flash of colour, a glimpse, and then they were gone, no matter how hard I craned my neck, shifted in my seat.

Gone. Until the evening. The big match.

A big match: the receptionist at the hotel had no idea was taking place, or any idea as to why someone – and someone who was neither Maltese nor Sammarinese to boot – would want to attend.

'Really?' she asked when I answered her question as to my plans that night, the look of surprise quickly turning to one of confusion, then concern, pity for her guest, smiling politely when I explained that I had seen the first match between the two a week ago in San Marino.

'Enjoy,' she said, with an uncertainty in her voice that suggested that the notion of enjoyment, football, Malta, and San Marino seemed a very abstract, and unlikely concept to her.

Abstract to her, but not those that were making their way to Ta' Qali beneath a setting sun – excitement as thick as the humidity, and clouds of mosquitos building among the growing dusk.

Excitement was building. Excitement, and something new. Something born out of the positive effect the Nations League has had in Malta – expectation.

In his interview in the match programme, national team head coach Devis Mangia – who had overseen a successful 2020 Nations League tournament, a positive World Cup qualifying campaign following that, two impressive friendly wins over Kuwait and Azerbaijan in March, and a narrow friendly defeat to Venezuela before this 2022 Nations League – addressed this new feeling.

Buoyed by the victory over San Marino, and the 94 minutes prior to Henry Anier's late winner for Estonia, Mangia urged his players to embrace this new emotion, not see it as a burden – something he thought had contributed to their slow start against San Marino.

'It is the result that the players must take into consideration, namely the fact that high expectations increase the level of recognition for this group of players and staff and the work done so far.
'We have made significant steps forward, there is no doubt about that, but this has to be a matter of pride rather than a source of added pressure.
'We need to strive for the best result possible. To be honest, I always demand this from our players, irrespective of the opposition, and I expect this in the UEFA Nations League group, nothing has changed.
'But, as I said, it has to be a matter of pride to be able to challenge for an important target and we can't perceive it in a different way. We have to perceive it as something that, collectively, we have constructed in these years and earn this recognition, that we can challenge for an important objective which could also turn into a historic landmark.'

Maybe that the players felt they had something else to play for this night helped to settle those nerves, the burden of increased expectation. Grief a more powerful emotion than anything.

Ta' Qali can hold 16,000 when one of the continent's giants pays a visit. As it is 2,646 have congregated in this bowl stadium, amassed in the two main stands either side of the half-way line. Only ball boys and girls populate the curved terracing behind each goal, scampering to retrieve wayward balls from last-minute practice shots by each nation's strikers.

The drums and trumpets, the tabards of the Maltese footballing knights from Serravalle are swelled by blocks of flag waving, scarf twirling support on the far side. Only three of the Sammarinese supporting Brigata Mai Una Gioia have made the trip, and stand, surrounded by their flags and banners in a swathe of empty seats high up behind the substitutes' benches. Applauding their heroes as they come out onto the pitch, they stand and wave from within in their self-imposed, blue and white nylon bank of segregation. National team flags and banners brilliant beneath the floodlights.

National anthems, that faraway look, bands of brothers, arms round each other's shoulders, ready for battle. But not before a moment to remember the fallen.

The Maltese players carry a picture of "Il-Lullu" across to the Maltese bench, hold it up to the crowd for a moment before placing it gently on the seat where Mark Piscopo would have sat. A pause, heads bowed, before they break and make for their positions on the pitch and wait for the referee's whistle.

Like the first half a week before, it is one of frustration for Malta. San Marino soak up the pressure and look to attack on the counter. And when Malta do break through and create a chance, there is Elia Benedettini to pull off a series of impressive saves. It is a composed performance from the visitors, who are able to lean on a lifetime of footballing backs-to-the-wall situations to soak up the pressure. But always, always with that attacking intent on their minds – Nicola Nanni and Andrea Grandoni buzzing about the front line, running into the channels every time San Marino reclaim the ball, looking for an opportunity to push forward.

Frustration once more for the Maltese. But, not long after half time, they get their breakthrough.

With only five minutes of the second half gone a wicked Ryan Camenzuli cross is met by right back Zach Muscat's head, who plants it past Benedettini for only his third goal for his country. The Maltese players make for the bench and "Il-Lullu's" picture, placing their hands on it, pointing to the sky.

Piscopo had been there for Muscat's international debut in 2014, at the Anton Malatinsky, Trnava, Slovakia in September 2014. He had been there for his first goal back in June 2017, at the Liebenauer Stadium, Graz, Austria in a one-nil friendly win over Ukraine. He had been there for his second in October 2021 at the Georgios Karapatakis AEK Stadium in Larnaca, Cyprus in a World Cup qualifier.

And to the players, to Muscat, it was clear that they felt he was still there. Would always be there as they looked up into the inky black night sky, framed so perfectly by the four floodlights that would have been so familiar to Piscopo during his 12 years as kit man, and lifetime as supporter.

A beautiful, poignant moment.

Malta pressed for a second, Benedettini pulling off four fantastic saves in short succession. But his best was reserved for a point-blank header from Teddy Teuma that seemed certain to bulge the back of the net.

It would have rounded off a great season for Teuma, who had won a runner's up medal in the Belgian Pro League with Royale Union Saint-Gilloise, helping his team qualify for Europe for the first time since 1964. But Benedettini had other ideas, and somehow clawed it out round the post and to safety – that had even the Maltese supporters applauding in begrudging respect for what they had just seen.

And with Benedettini's heroics, San Marino were inspired. They were still in this game. And when Malta missed an open goal in the 80th minute, San Marino turned the screw.

A counterattack, a through ball, right-back Allesandro D'Addario – himself coming off the back of a successful season for his club Tre Fiori, where he helped them qualify for Europe as well by winning the Coppa

Titano – bore down on goal. A vicious strike that had Henry Bonello in the Maltese goal beaten.

Time seemed to stand still.

The Sammarinese bench, having risen to their feet as one, frozen in anticipation, the Brigata Mai Una Gioia, arms raised above their heads watched, waited.

The ball smacked the base of the post with such force that it shot back out and away from goal as quickly as it had arrived, clattering into the advertising hoardings and safety for a throw-in.

The Sammarinese bench, as one, sank to the ground, prostrate. So close.

The Brigata Mai Una Gioia, within the width of a lick of paint to that oh so very illusive joy, stood bent double, hands on knees, as if they had been punched in the stomach. Air expelled from their lungs.

But there was no time for that.

The Maltese were wobbling, and, as the clock ran down, San Marino were through on goal once more. But in their desperation to capitalise they took an extra touch, just long enough for Malta to claw their way back into position, cut off the cross to an unmarked Nicola Nanni.

And by those finest of margins, the final whistle brought jubilation and abject desperation in equal measure.

No matter which side of the emotional fence you landed, it had been a thrilling, captivating match. The drama, endeavour and skill on display inspiring, as seen in the excited chatter of young children while families filed away from Ta' Qali – the grand walls of Mdina looming in the darkness beyond.

It had been a victory for Malta. That momentum maintained. It had been a victory for Mark "Il-Lullu" Piscopo. It had been a victory in instilling in the children of Malta a new definition of what their country can be, on and off the football pitch.

Even to the Sammarinese, applauding the Brigata up in the stands, it had been a moral victory – progression, something most definitely to build upon. A good performance all over the pitch.

Fortune favours the brave. And one day, soon, that bravery will surely bear fruit.

Just not today.

Shoulders drooped as they trudged off the pitch. The sounds of car horns honking outside, trumpets blaring, drums beating, chanting, the hum of excitement.

One day it will all be theirs. A product of *their* hard work, solidified in statistic, with that illusive win.

Momentum is building…

Back in Valletta, the bars and restaurants around the main squares are doing great business. Tables spill out beneath canopies onto the pavement. Conversation, laughter, weave among them along with busy waiters carrying menus, bottles of wine, plates of food.

In the background of every bar, every restaurant, on televisions mounted behind the counter, and projected onto screens, the same scene is being broadcast.

As you walk past each establishment the image on the screen follows you with a smooth continuity, and a new-found familiarity as commentators talk pitch-side at Ta' Qali. Brilliant beneath the floodlights, these muted pundits gesticulate in front of now deserted stands, their expertise intercut with clips of the match.

Tired-looking barmen slouch against the beer taps and watch absently this silent deconstruction of a game that most diners barely recognised was on. The occasional pause to focus in on the abbreviated names of the teams and the scoreline in the top left hand of the screen. A shake of the head, a shrug of the shoulders at the unfamiliar "Mal – San" shortform, and the players that represented them, the badges on their shirts. Out of context, the repeats of Zach Muscat's header, the gaggle of players holding up a photograph, pointing to the sky, passes by largely ignored. The meaning lost. Or never known in the first place.

It is a pity, as 90 minutes at Ta' Qali seems as vital a cultural signifier, as much a champion of Maltese culture as the museums and monuments, churches and megalithic temples.

Just like the families sitting around the makeshift café bar among the stone beach huts clinging to the harbours edge, children by the water, watching lights twinkling on the dead calm sea. Following little fishing boats chugging out into the darkness.

Just like the wedding party in the park above, singing and dancing beneath strings of fairy lights. Just like the woman, lost in a moment at the door to the church that morning, the actions and reactions of those on the pitch and in the stands at the national stadium, are as much the true soul of Malta as anything in a guidebook.

And they play out, whether anyone is noticing or not. And they always will. Across this ancient, timeless landscape.

And, for now, for its football supporters, they slip away into the humid Mediterranean night with the satisfaction in a victory well-won. And something even more precious. Beyond a bolstered pride in your team, your nation, who you are and where you are from.

They leave Ta' Qali with a sense of hope.
For the next fixture. And beyond.
"Il-Lullu" would be very happy.

Line-ups: 12.06.22, National Stadium, Ta' Qali

Malta

1 Henry Bonello
3 Ryan Camenzuli
5 Ferdinando Apap (Jean Borg 78')
6 Matthew Guillaumier ©
7 Joseph Mbong
9 Luke Montebello (Alexander Satariano 87')
11 Brandon Paiber (Dunston Vella 78')
13 Enrico Pepe
17 Teddy Teuma
20 Luke Gambin (Jurgen Degabriele 71')
22 Zach Muscat (1)

San Marino

23 Elia Benedettini
2 Allesandro D'Addario (Tommaso Zafferani 79')
3 Mirko Palazzi ©
4 Luca Ceccaroli (Adolfo José Hirsch 79')
8 Michael Battistini
9 Nicola Nanni
11 Dante Rossi
13 Andrea Grandoni (Danilo Rinaldi 61')
17 Filippo Fabbri
19 David Tomassini (Marcello Mularoni 61')
21 Lorenzo Lunadei (Matteo Vitaioli 85')

Nations League D Group Two

02.06.22 – Estonia 2 San Marino 0
05.06.22 – San Marino 0 Malta 2
09.06.22 – Malta 1 Estonia 2
12.06.22 – Malta 1 San Marino 0

	P	W	D	L	F	A	Pts
Estonia	2	2	0	0	4	1	6
Malta	3	2	0	1	4	2	6
San Marino	3	0	0	3	0	5	0

Chapter Four – Latvia v Moldova
September 22, 2022

PEOPLE WHO SAY "sport and Politics should not mix" are usually the sort of people who have a vested interest in keeping politics out of sport. And by "vested interest" read "have an opportunity to make a lot of money if politics, morality, and reality, can be kept out of it."

Politics does not want to be in sport, but sometimes has no choice if those running sport make dubious decisions. Of which there are many examples.

Handing the world's greatest sporting events to regimes and faux democracies with appalling human rights records can be a money-spinner if the optics can be handled. And those optics are usually framed by declaring that the feeling of inclusion a nation receives by hosting the Olympics, the World Cup, will inevitably bring about positive change and harmony.

The diversity of religion, race, sexuality, personal freedoms of expression imported through competitors, spectators, sponsors will broaden horizons and create a lasting legacy.

A legacy that will help nations with a history of repression, subjugation, and intolerance find a new path toward enlightenment and acceptance among the global community.

That is the theory. And while the theory is tested, lots of money is made. And once the theory has been proven, the circus has already moved on. On towards the next potential pay-day.

And so, the cycle continues.

In the years since Beijing hosted the Olympic Games in 2008, the Chinese Government have increased its programme of erasing Buddhism, eradicating the influence of the Dalai Lama, and the culture and history of the Tibetans in their occupied land by imposing re-education programmes, forced relocation, and harsh prison sentences for any perceived dissent.

Perceived dissent can include owning a photograph of the Dalai Lama, questioning Chinese Government policy, and performing certain religious or cultural ceremonies.

Increasingly in Tibet, self-immolation is the last form of protest open to those who feel hopeless enough to take this route.

Meanwhile, in Xinjiang in northwestern China, the Muslim Uyghur population are suffering similar forced re-education programmes, with more than one million detained in this way. Amnesty International and

Human Rights Watch, along with many UN members including the USA have also accused the Chinese Government of genocide and crimes against humanity against the Uyghurs.

Since 2014, in Hong Kong, new draconian laws have prevented Hong Kongers from self-governance. Freedoms of speech, movement, and association have been curtailed with police beatings, severe prison sentences and extradition to mainland China.

And right now, the waters around Taiwan are building up with war ships, the threat of Chinese invasion looming…

In 2018 Russia hosted the World Cup despite supporting a purge on the LGBT community in Chechnya that began a year before the tournament. Unlawful detentions, beatings, sexual humiliation and torture by electric shock were commonplace.

Just three months before the tournament began, Russia carried out the poisoning of dual Russian and British nationals Sergei and Julia Skripal in Salisbury using the deadly nerve agent Novichok. Both Sergei and Julia, along with Detective Sergeant Nick Bailey, who was exposed to the agent while searching the Skripal's home, were rushed to hospital.

He wouldn't leave hospital for three weeks. For Sergei it took three months.

On the June 30th, a day before Russia's round of 16 victory over Spain, Charlie Rowley and Dawn Sturgess were exposed to the poison when they discovered the bottle that had been used to carry it to the UK.

On July 8, the day after Russia's defeat to Croatia in the quarter finals, Dawn Sturgess died from her exposure to Novichok.

Fresh from the glow of a successful tournament, the rehabilitation of Russia's image began in earnest a year later with the banning of all Russian athletes from competing at the Olympic games due to the discovery of a systematic programme of doping across all sports.

And less than three years after that, and before the next edition of the World Cup, Russia's newly forged renaissance within the international community – thanks to being able to host such a prestigious event as football's premiere spectacle – was solidified with the full-scale invasion of Ukraine.

Sport and politics do not mix, until they do. And invasion of a fellow member state of the UN, UEFA, and FIFA meant that it was unavoidable. Russia was banned from all UEFA and FIFA sanctioned competition.

Fifty-five member states became 54 for the 2022 edition of the Nations League.

And for those nations bordering Russia and Ukraine – nations now with war on their doorstep – fear, uncertainty, the trauma of previously lived experience, the weight of that modern history, and nervous glances to the east peppered their every waking thought.

Nations like Latvia and Moldova, who, but for the grace of geography, could have been in Ukraine's position – after all, both have been declared targets, just like Ukraine, in Putin's aim to reclaim the former Russian Empire.

Their modern histories run parallel with each other, Latvia, Moldova, Ukraine.

Latvia had declared independence from the fallen German Empire after World War I but were forcibly incorporated into the Soviet Union in 1939 via the Molotov-Ribbentrop Pact.

A treaty of non-aggression between Germany and the Soviet Union, swathes of Europe, were carved up and divided between the two to help guarantee peace. Latvia was incorporated into the Soviet Union. The Molotov-Ribbentrop pact failed when Germany invaded and occupied Latvia in 1941 – during which time more than 200,000 Latvians were killed, including the extermination of some 75,000 Latvian Jews as part of the final solution.

Germany held the country until the Soviets re-occupied it in 1944.

After the war, the Latvian Soviet Socialist Republic was established, which stood until the collapse of the Soviet Union, and Latvia finally gained independence once more in August 1991.

Moldova, or Bessarabia as it was known then, also declared independence from the old-world order after World War I. In 1918 it declared itself autonomous and chose to form an alliance with neighbour Wallachia to create the first iteration of Romania.

But in 1924 Soviet Russia declared Bessarabia a part of the Moldavian Autonomous Region, which became a part of the Ukrainian Soviet Socialist Republic.

In 1939 the Molotov-Ribbentrop Pact formally assigned the region to the Soviets, and the Moldavian Soviet Socialist Republic was formed.

And as the Soviet Union collapsed, the MSSR declared independence, again in August 1991, naming itself Moldova.

Ukraine, like Latvia, had once been a part of the old Czarist Russian Empire, but after the Russian Revolution it declared independence in 1917 as the Ukrainian People's Republic. But as the Bolsheviks, lead by Lenin, consolidated control over much of the former Russian Empire, Ukraine was once again drawn back in, becoming the Ukrainian Soviet Socialist Republic in 1922.

Like Lativa, Ukraine was invaded and occupied by Nazi Germany during World War II.

Seven million Ukrainians were killed, and almost the entire Jewish Ukrainian community were exterminated before the Soviet Union pushed back the Germans in late 1944.

In August 1991, within days of Latvia and Moldova, Ukraine declared independence once more upon the collapse of the Soviet Union.

Ukraine's current pain and suffering is acutely felt by those who have been made to endure similarly, often within living memory. And in September 2022 that pain is everywhere you turn in Riga, Latvia's capital. Pain, but also fear, and no small amount of anger.

September in the Baltic states is a time of contradiction. Blue, cloudless skies reveal a sun that feels warm on the skin. Young people meet up in the parks, lounging in the warmth, watching the old trams clack and clatter on and into Riga old town. Beautiful wooden canal-boats chug quietly along a winding waterway that meanders through the parks carrying handfuls of tourists, before turning out and onto the great Daugava River that leads in one direction out into the Baltic Sea, the other past a beautiful city-scape of glistening church spires, parliament buildings, presidential residences, and grand municipal institutions harbouring Latvia's cultural and artistic legacy, all shimmering in the sun.

But venture into the shade of the grand old trees in the sprawling parks, the shadow of a building, or the freedom monument honouring the soldiers killed during the war of Independence from 1918 to 1920, and you feel a chill.

There is a sharp, fresh bite to the air, reminding you that winter is coming. And with it, not so very far away, a brutal, desperate battle is still playing out. A battle that will become attritional as the ground freezes and the snow begins to fall. A battle that could yet become your battle.

After all, no-one truly believed Putin would invade Ukraine…

Behind the veneer of everyday life in Riga, the invasion of Ukraine is everywhere. The Blue and yellow flag of Ukraine flies from lamp posts, hangs in windows, has been painted on walls across the city. Blue and yellow ribbons flutter in tree branches. Posters of Volodymyr Zelensky adorn shop windows. Given such a display of solidarity it is hard to believe that you are not actually in Ukraine itself.

The national colours of Ukraine a resounding show of support, but also a manifestation of the fear felt by a population who knew all too well the drab, colourless existence of a life under Russian occupation. With identity neutered, reassigned. Symbols drained of colour, made obsolete.

And in Kronvalda Park, opposite the Russian Embassy, the largest, most colourful and unambiguous of protests has been erected.

A forest of white flag poles, like a dense copse of silver birch trees, host a swath of Ukrainian flags that flutter and snap on the breeze. Beneath them, an old upright piano painted in yellow and blue stands by, ready for the daily gathering of people who come, play the Ukrainian national anthem, popular Ukrainian folk and protest songs that can't help but be heard from within the Russian Embassy compound.

And if the odd staffer came out when it was quiet, crossed the street and took a look at the large wall that had been erected for people to write messages of support, they would surely appreciate that the vast majority of their host nation was horrified, scared, and angry at Russia's actions.

If that didn't, then the vast banner hung on a residential block next door most certainly would.

More than three storeys tall, and important enough for residents to give up their daylight from obscured windows, it depicted Putin, his face dissolving from a typically stoic, steely-eyed pose into that of a skeleton. Teeth and cheekbones exposed, it was a chilling sight, staring across at the windows of the embassy. A message that the point of no return had been reached. That there could be no going back. For him or Latvia, Ukraine, Moldova.

There could be no life under Russian rule. And no place for Putin if his grand plan failed.

And just as the protest could leave no-one within the Russian embassy in any doubt as to which side of history the Latvians believed they were on, it served as a morale booster for the embattled staff of the Ukrainian embassy, just three doors further down the street.

While countrymen, women, children were being killed back home, while villages, towns, cities were being reduced to rubble, invaded, subsumed illegally into newly Russian-controlled territories of Luhansk, Donetsk, Kherson, and Zaporizhzia, an unfathomable tension played out across less than 50 metres of pavement.

A row of police cars, lights flashing day and night, separate the two embassies. Officers stand outside each entrance and dot the gap between, in ones and twos. While relatives are living and dying back home, civility, diplomacy must continue. Bumping into staffers of the other in the local market, a coffee shop, having to be met with a blank, emotionless expression, pretending not to notice them.

Should the worst happen, should Kyiv, Zelensky fall, and their embassy became the mission of a country that had, overnight, simply disappeared from the world, what would happen then? To the police protection, the safety of the embassy grounds?

Life, identity erased.

Recent history told of how that would look and feel. After all, by September 2022 it had only been 31 years since independence from the last Russian Empire.

And the national football team, or the painful lack of it, is as visceral an example of what life under occupation, life without identity can feel like.

A life Latvia has known all too well.

After independence following World War I, the Latvian Football Federation were formed in 1921, joining FIFA a year later. Their first international match on 24th September 1922 was against neighbours Estonia, which finished in a one-all draw.

Competitive football began in 1928 with the inaugural Baltic Cup, featuring fellow Baltic nations Lithuania and Estonia. Latvia would win the first edition, with further victories in 1932, 1936, and 1937.

Those victories in 1936 and 1937 paved the way for a first ever World Cup qualifying campaign.

A qualifying campaign like no other, it featured some remarkable groups and teams.

Germany, competing in the World Cup for the first and last time under the Swastika, came out on top of a group containing Sweden, Estonia and Finland.

The Irish Free State (that would become the Republic of Ireland) also took part, narrowly losing out to Norway.

Mandatory Palestine, also known as "Land of Israel National Football Team," represented the British Mandate of Palestine, though was almost entirely comprised from the Jewish community that made up a fifth of the population at the time. They lost home and away to Greece, while a ridiculous qualifying group featuring Romania and Egypt was resolved when Egypt withdrew after objecting to having to play during the holy month of Ramadan.

Latvia meanwhile showed great promise with comfortable four-two and five-one wins over Lithuania before a narrow two-one defeat to an Austrian team who had finished fourth at the 1934 World Cup, losing their semi-final one-nil to eventual winners Italy.

It was a promise that would never be given the opportunity to materialise.

In 1938 Ēriks Raisters would score the last competitive goal for Latvia for more than 53 years in a one-all draw with Estonia in the Baltic Cup.

As tensions rose, Raisters, along with his Latvian team-mates would only play three friendlies in 1939 – in Bucharest against Romania for a four-nil loss on 18 May, a three-nil defeat in Sofia six days later against Bulgaria, and a last home game for 52 years with a three-all draw in July against Estonia (who would also be the first team they would play in 1991 after independence from Soviet rule).

His, and every Latvian player's final ever appearance for their country came on 18 July 1940 in Tallin, where a two-one loss – the 99th official Latvian National Team match – called time on the team, and the country as an independent entity, as the Molotov-Ribbentrop Pact saw Latvia absorbed into the Soviet Union.

And with that Latvia, and the Latvian National Football Team were no more.

Ēriks Raisters became the perfect allegory for life under Soviet occupation.

Having made 27 appearances for his national team and playing for the best team in the land – RFK Riga, Raisters' life and career would be taken out of his hands.

With no national team to play for, and his club side disbanded (as all had been) he was selected to play for FK Dinamo Riga within the Soviet football system.

Then, in early 1941, the exiled Latvian free press reported that Ēriks had been involved in a conflict with a representative of the Soviet occupation authorities. He was put on trial, found guilty, whereby the court sentenced him to either serve nine years imprisonment, or to play for Dinamo Minsk in Belarus.

Nine years in a Soviet gulag was as good as a death sentence, so Raisters agreed to play for Dinamo, which he did six times in the Spring of 1941 before he was drafted into the Red Army.

While he served in the trenches, Ēriks contracted tuberculosis and died on 25 May 1942 in an army camp in Gorohovica, 1270 kilometres from Riga.

He was buried in a cemetery in the nearby village of Zalina.

He was 28.

All he had wanted to do was play football and represent his country.

Fifty-one long years passed for the Latvian Soviet Socialist Republic. Fifty-one long years without being able to celebrate a national identity, or a national football team. Until August 1991.

No time was wasted, and within three months the first Baltic Cup since 1938 took place in Lithuania between the three newly independent countries.

On 19 November 1991, in front of 200 spectators at the Žalgiris Stadium, Klaipéda, Dzintars Sproģis scored the first Latvian goal since Raisters' all those years before in a two-nil win.

It was a result that barely registered beyond the Baltics and doesn't, to this day, as a FIFA sanctioned fixture. But the significance of it, and what it represented was profound.

Three nations had their identities, and their national teams back.

A first FIFA-recognised match came in April 1992 with a two-nil defeat against Romania. And with that, Latvia began a period of slow and steady progress on the international scene, helped in no small part by the impact of Marian Pahars on the English Premier League.

"The Latvian Michael Owen" as he was called was parachuted into a seemingly doomed Southampton side in April 1999, and with no time to acclimatise to his new surroundings he scored the goals that kept the Saints in the Premier League.

The following season he carried on where he had left off, famously nut-megging one of the best defenders in world football at the time, Jaap Stam, at Old Trafford in a game against Manchester United.

A Pahars inspired Latvian National team went on to do something that no other team in League D of the Nations League has ever done – qualify for a major tournament.

In 2003 Latvia beat Turkey in a play-off and qualified for the 2004 European Championship where they lost to the Czech Republic two-one, the Netherlands three-nil, and drew with Germany nil-nil.

An injured Marian Pahars battled back to some kind of fitness, and played a cameo role in each game, coming off the bench.

But as Pahars' injury-prone career wound down after the Euros of 2004, the Latvian National Team kept on, narrowly missing out on qualification to the 2010 World Cup, where a five-two defeat to their group rivals Greece ended any hope of progress.

Such a brutal defeat, so close to achieving the ultimate in football, seemed to create a trauma in Latvian football. A hangover that resulted in a sharp decline in form, culminating in a Euro 2020 qualifying campaign where they lost nine of their ten games. And by the time the Nations League was created, Latvia had cemented themselves among the teams that would make up League D.

In 2018 their first outing in the Nations League saw them come third behind Georgia and Kazakhstan with no wins to their name. In 2020 they fared slightly better, coming third behind the Faroe Islands and Malta.

But with at least a victory to celebrate in a last day win over Andorra, and four draws out of their six games, progress was being made. Confidence was being rebuilt.

Confidence that saw their 2022 Nations League campaign unfold with victory after victory.

A three-nil win over Andorra on 3 June was followed up three days later with a one-nil success against Liechtenstein. Then, on 10 June, an impressive four-two away win against Moldova (where visiting teams had to get the train in, as Moldovan airspace had been considered too dangerous with Russia advancing on the Ukrainian city of Odessa not far from the Moldovan border), and a two-nil win in Vaduz over Lichtenstein saw Latvia take complete control of League D, Group One.

Just one more win, against their closest rivals Moldova on 22 September would see Latvia begin that long road back to where they had once been with a first step, and promotion up into League C.

Riga old town glistens. Lovingly maintained old townhouses painted in pastel shades of orange, lemon, light blue, mint, mingle with grand churches, municipal buildings that look like old museums, restaurants and bars cloistered in basements and courtyards, even the presidential residence of Riga Castle, all bound together along narrow streets, some cobbled and untouched since medieval times.

They glow in the last throes of an Indian summer that is warm and inviting in the sun, but chill, chastening, in the shade. The grand Daugava River shimmers, its glare overwhelming the little tourist boats that chug up and back, but the cool breeze off it reminds everyone that this will not last. Winter is coming.

Beneath the imposing St. Peter's Church, with views from its steeple across town and into the forested Latvian interior, old men set up stalls of their paintings: the tall, thin construction of the townhouses, exaggerated slightly, looming over narrow, cobbled, deserted alleys. They are beautiful, arresting, and ten euros to anyone that shows an interest.

Bars, restaurants, cafes, extend from beneath awnings, pushing out across narrow cobbled pathways with rows of tables and chairs to make the most of the sun. From within, and without, a laid-back bustle feels relaxed, benign, in no great hurry. Among such old, timeless buildings, adorned with beautiful flowering clematis creeping up towards top floor town house windows, stunning murals detailing the vibrant crests of each of Latvia's towns and regions, and splashes of pastel colour among ageing beams and lattice, it seems a shame to have to hurry.

Tourists join this lethargic flow happily, lingering to look up at the architecture, taking a seat outside one of the establishments to drink in the scenery as well as a coffee or a beer.

Riga old town appears idyllic. A picture postcard at every turn, it's beautiful architecture largely untouched for centuries, it is perhaps no great surprise that, like its predecessors in Valletta and San Marino City, it is a UNESCO World Heritage Site.

No matter what you may think of the football on offer in League D of the Nations League, it is most certainly League A in beauty, history, and culture.

But among that beauty, there is tension.

After more than 50 years of Soviet occupation, it is perhaps no great surprise that Russians comprise the largest minority group in Latvia. And thanks to Putin's invasion of Ukraine, and the groundswell of support for Volodymyr Zelensky and his embattled country, those who have made Latvia home are in a kind of limbo.

Among the sea of Ukrainian flags and ribbons, banners of the Russian leader in an advanced state of decomposition, protest gatherings, sanctions on the motherland, and a universal groundswell of horror and outrage at Putin's actions, those of Russian descent walk on eggshells.

People turn their coat collars up to hide their faces as they enter the Russian embassy for visas, or any other form of consular support.

The beautiful Russian Orthodox church, with its glistening golden domes and the intoxicating smell of incense drifting down the steps of the main entrance is populated by people who hurry, head down, up those steps and inside to pray.

The lighting of incense, protestations before statues, bowing of heads and signing of the cross hurried, as if staying too long was no longer a good idea. That any open display of Russian-hood of any kind was to be curtailed as much as possible, whether through a shared sense of horror and despair, or a new-found fear where there hadn't been before.

One man's actions throwing the lives of millions of Ukrainians, and the Russian diaspora in the Baltics and beyond into turmoil.

The tension around these Russian institutions was palpable. Though, as game time approached, and thoughts turned to the national team, tension around Riga began to give way to excitement, hope, expectation at the imminent redemption of their football team.

Skonto Stadium was abuzz, as a sold-out crowd of 7,000 queued to get in. Children lined-up to get their faces painted in the dark red (or a carmine-red) and white colours of the Latvian flag. A DJ played big-beat dance anthems at an ear-bleeding level, while the national team mascot, a seven-foot wolf with maniacal eyes, dressed up in a Latvian team kit virtually crowd-surfed up and back across the rows of seats in the main stand to high-five/terrify children in equal measure.

Elsewhere, on the concourse beneath the stand, children queued up to buy Latvia scarves, t-shirts, national team kit, pictures of their heroes from a merchandise stall under siege by a sea of expectant and excited faces. Fists clutching euro notes of varying denominations, handed down to them by parents who had enjoyed the beer stand enough to offer a little extra to their pleading offspring. Strong Baltic lager, and a pride in how desperate their children were to show off their national colours – to collect their Latvian heroes in postcard form – releasing a few extra notes on this evening of celebration.

After all, this moment had been a long time in coming. Twelve long years of terminal decline finally arrested. Just one more win to gain promotion up into League C.

As the players came out for the national anthems, the sky lit up with a stunning sunset of reds, oranges, and pinks, illuminating the cloud cover in a fantastic display, like a biblical painting of a miracle in progress. Some divine message that this night was to be special. Finally delivering Latvian football from the wilderness…

Moldova's first goal came on 26 minutes. Ioan-Călin Revenco meeting a brilliant cross by Sergiu Platica, powering home a header to score his first ever goal for his country, sending the 20 Moldovan supporters who had made the long trip into raptures.

It had been a trip made in hope rather than expectation. A display of pride in their team, their nation, who they were, that had brought them to Riga, huddled in the far corner behind a small display of Moldovan flags draped across the advertising hoardings in front of them.

After all, like Latvia, the actions and intent of Putin were to eventually snuff out Moldova as an independent country. Their flag, their national football team, their identity consigned to history.

And as they celebrated Revenco's goal, jumping up and down, twirling scarves above their heads, they knew, back home, that Ukrainians continued to flee across the border into Moldova as Russia advanced upon Odessa – the last city and line of defence in Ukraine that stood between the war and Moldova itself.

Supporting their team, celebrating Moldovan nationhood, even in small numbers seemed, now more than ever, vital. Celebrating a goal even more so.

If they were in raptures with the first goal, they were in dreamland just before half time when another probing run down the wing ended with another wicked cross, and another pin-point header, this time by Ion Nicolaescu to put Moldova two-nil up.

Like Latvia, Malta, and all the countries in League D of the Nations League, scoring away from home was, in the most part, a rarity.

It was not expected, even if it was hoped for, so these moments of celebration were to be cherished, which is exactly what Moldova's tiny band of brothers and sisters did – leaping for joy, nearly tumbling over the advertising hoardings as they hugged one another, punched the air, twirled their scarves, seemingly attempting all three at the same time. They were still recovering when the half-time whistle went, but had enough breath left to cheer their heroes off the pitch, basking in the dreamland of a two-goal lead away from home.

Around them, among the home support, half time wasn't maybe as subdued as it should have been. Children chased the wolf mascot up and down in front of the main stand, and the bar kept doing a roaring trade with smiling faces, groups of friends enjoying each other's company.

Possibly the war had helped put footballing concerns into perspective. Maybe also the fact that Latvia had actually played well, despite conceding two, and that their four straight wins in the group meant that only two Moldovan wins, and two heavy Latvian defeats in these final two rounds could deny Latvia their destiny.

That philosophical mindset was rewarded just ten minutes into the second half when Jānis Ikaunieks drilled a shot past Dumitru Celeadnic in the Moldovan goal from the edge of the penalty area, sending the wolf mascot and his pack of children around him pogo-ing with joy, while the stands behind them rose to their feet in a guttural roar. Latvian goals, just like Moldovan ones, were also hoped for, not expected – even on such a good run of form. And an outpouring of pride reverberated up into the night sky as Ikaunieks punched the air, waved into the stands, ran purposely back to the half-way line. Neither him nor his Latvian teammates wanted to settle for one.

For Ikaunieks, his teammates, the wolf mascot and his entourage trailing behind him, they would, however, have to.

And despite Moldova holding on beneath a Latvian barrage on their goal, moods had not been dampened on the final whistle.

For the Moldovans, celebrating with hugs and high-fives with their small band of supporters, and the Latvians, who applauded all sides of the Skonto stadium – who had stayed on to cheer and inspire their heroes for one last push away in Andorra – it had been a positive experience.

Both teams expressed themselves and played with attacking intent.

Performances to be proud of.

Performances to build upon.

But also, there was a sense of gratitude, among the supporters and the players. Gratitude that this game was taking place at all, that the aggression, the will to win, was the only thing of concern.

It was not lost on anyone that Ukraine – who were so similar to Moldova and Latvia in their histories, and their importance in Putin's vision for a restored Russian empire – could only take part in their Nations League, League B campaign, by playing all their home games in Poland. Their homeland being unsafe to host international football, and where their domestic league is played behind closed doors, and exiled teams from towns and cities on the frontline of the war having to relocate to the west of the country. Representing places being bombed, sometimes out of existence, such as Mariupol.

It is hard to bemoan a defeat in the Nations League with your Ukrainian friends enduring so much. And fighting to help preserve not only their country, but those who would be next if Ukraine fell. Nations like Latvia and Moldova.

Sometimes footballing rivalry, the desire to win can be put into perspective.

The satisfaction of a good performance in defeat, a good performance in victory becoming more than enough. Being played out in the safety of a free and fair country.

The memory of that gap between Ēriks Raisters' goal in 1938 to Latvia's next one courtesy of Dzintars Sproģis in 1991 enough to help instil a perspective that other nations may lack in the face of sporting defeat.

Sometimes the very act of representing your nation, supporting your nation, celebrating your identity through face paint, delirious-looking mascots, replica shirts and scarves matters more than three points, or promotion. And more than ever with war raging in the east.

As the 7,000 filed out and into the chill Baltic night, it was that sense of perspective that accompanied them. A warm glow from your team giving it everything, enough to sustain you until next time.

Football is a matter of life and death, until it isn't.

Sport and politics should never mix. Until they must.

And for Latvia, having to wait three more days to secure promotion. In the face of everything going on in the world, that was not so much to ask.

Patience is a virtue. And that virtue was rewarded in Andorra with a one-all draw – which was so very nearly a win but for an 88th minute equaliser by the hosts.

That point rendered Moldova's last gasp victory over Liechtenstein a case of too little, too late. The group was Latvia's, and with it, promotion to League C and a new challenge against Armenia, the Faroe Islands, and North Macedonia that would begin in September 2024.

Only time would tell as to what kind of Europe these fixtures would be played in.

Only time would tell if Ukraine would still be a part of UEFA and the free world. And if Latvia and Moldova had themselves been moved one step closer to invasion, conflict…

Line-ups: 22.09.22, Skonto Stadium, Riga

Latvia

1 Pāvels Šteinbors
3 Kristers Tobers
4 Kaspars Dubra
5 Antonijs Černomordijs ©
8 Eduards Emsis
9 Vladislavs Gutkovskis
10 Jānis Ikaunieks (1)
11 Roberts Savalnieks
13 Raivis Jurkovskis (Elvis Struglis 88')
14 Andrejs Cigaņiks (Dāvis Ikaunieks 82')
16 Alvis Jaunzems (Raimonds Krollis 57')

Moldova

1 Dumitru Celeadnic
4 Igor Armaș
5 Veaceslav Posmac
7 Artur Ioniță ©
8 Nichita Moțpan (Eugeniu Cociuc 84')
9 Ion Nicolaescu (1) (Virgiliu Postolachi 73')
11 Vitalie Damașcan (Maxim Cojocaru 90')
13 Mihail Caimacov
14 Artur Craicun
20 Sergiu Platica (Ion Jardan 84')
21 Ioan-Călin Revenco (1)

Nations League D Group One

03.06.22 – Latvia 3 Andorra 0
03.06.22 – Liechtenstein 0 Moldova 2
06.06.22 – Latvia 1 Liechtenstein 0
06.06.22 – Andorra 0 Moldova 0
10.06.22 – Moldova 2 Latvia 4
10.06.22 – Andorra 2 Liechtenstein 1
14.06.22 – Moldova 2 Andorra 1
14.06.22 – Liechtenstein 0 Latvia 2
22.09.22 – Latvia 1 Moldova 2
22.09.22 – Liechtenstein 0 Andorra 2
25.09.22 – Andorra 1 Latvia 1
25.09.22 – Moldova 2 – Liechtenstein 0

	P	W	D	L	F	A	Pts
Latvia	6	4	1	1	12	5	13
Moldova	6	4	1	1	10	6	13
Andorra	6	2	2	2	6	7	8
Liechtenstein	6	0	0	6	1	10	0

In Group 2, the League D Baltic domination was completed with Estonia's two victories in the September Nations League window.

Another late Henri Anier goal beat Malta two-one in Tallin – his goal this time arriving eight minutes earlier than his strike at Ta' Qali, coming in the 86th minute.

With the league and promotion secured, Anier would add two more to his tally in a final day win over San Marino in Serravalle.

Their four-nil victory being the biggest in League D, it would also bring down the curtain on the Nations League career of Sammarinese keeper Elia Benedettini.

He would, however, go on to play in nine of the ten San Marino Euro 2024 qualifying games from March to November 2023, including in two of the last three that would create another little Sammarinese fable as the Titans scored in three consecutive games for the first ever time.

He tended goal on 17 October in Serravalle when Alessandro Golinucci scored a 61st minute equaliser against a Denmark side featuring Schmeichel, Kjaer, Eriksen, Højberg, and Højlund – Benedettini racing the length of the pitch to join in the celebrations. A two-one defeat to the eventual group winners a mini-fable all its own.

On 17 November Benedettini would bear witness to Simone Franciosi's 60th minute strike in Astana, Kazakhstan – silencing a crowd of 30,000 that would only find it's voice again in the 92nd minute after a late Abat Aymbetov penalty, struck past Elia, took the game beyond San Marino, securing a three-one win.

He would watch on from the substitutes bench three days later in Serravalle as Filippo Berardi's 97th minute penalty would be the last action in the final match of the campaign, the Sammarinese losing two-one to Finland, but creating another piece of history, another fable.

Three games, three goals. For the first time ever.

Whether he knew it then, sat on the bench, that he would never represent his country again, that he would retire before the next round of matches in March 2024, we don't know.

It is likely that, in the excitement of Filippo's goal, in history being made – Sammarinese style – that even he didn't know that this would be it.

That final moment, to take it all in, savour it, one last time, gone. Lost in the moment.

A moment, it can be argued, forged from the positive experience of the Nations League. Instilling a belief, an edge to their play, that they *can* compete, these "amateurs of San Marino," even though the odds are so very much stacked against them. A belief that had them play out close games against Northern Ireland and Slovenia, followed up by those final three matches where they came so close to a positive result, and a European qualifying point.

And at this parting of the ways – Benedettini and the national team – a sense of great satisfaction could be found on both sides. One has benefitted the other, achieved more than maybe they ever dared dream.

Building foundations for the future. Foundations toward that seemingly impossible milestone – a competitive victory.

Foundations, belief, that maybe, just maybe, the impossible is not quite so unachievable after all.

Not a bad legacy, not a bad fable to leave behind, for others to take up – the career of Elia Benedettini.

All eyes turn to the Nations League, 2024…

Nations League D Group Two

02.06.22 – Estonia 2 San Marino 0
05.06.22 – San Marino 0 Malta 2
09.06.22 – Malta 1 Estonia 2
12.06.22 – Malta 1 San Marino 0
23.09.22 – Estonia 2 Malta 1
26.09.22 – San Marino 0 Estonia 4

	P	W	D	L	F	A	Pts
Estonia	4	4	0	0	10	2	12
Malta	4	2	0	2	5	4	6
San Marino	4	0	0	4	0	9	0

Chapter Five – Fifty-four Minus Three

THE GAP BETWEEN the mighty and the minnows in the men's game can be huge. Though thanks to FIFA and UEFA initiatives, funding programmes, excellent work by national associations and local clubs from the grassroots up, combined with competitions like the Nations League, these gaps are reducing.

Where defeats by eight or nine goals, sometimes more, used to be commonplace in men's international football, they are now an anomaly. Nations like Turkey, Iceland and Luxembourg, who routinely suffered heavy defeats in the seventies and eighties now qualify, or very nearly qualify for World Cups and European Championships.

And the true minnows of Europe, they can hold the likes of Denmark to narrow victories, can score in three consecutive games against respected opposition. Can, from time to time, almost bridge that gap completely. In the men's game.

It is a different story in the women's.

It is only in the last 15 years that the women's game has seen some of that desire by governing bodies to broaden the sport, enhance the competition, and create opportunity. Decades of inactivity, even open hostility to the women's game, and a woeful lack of funding has created a chasm between those UEFA members at the vanguard of the women's game, and those left behind.

In qualification for the 2023 World Cup, these disparities were writ large across some eye-watering results, where France beat Estonia 11-0, as did Northern Ireland in beating North Macedonia.

The Netherlands beat Cyprus 12-0, with one of the world's brightest talents in Vivianne Miedema scoring six.

Eventual World Cup winners Spain beat the Faroe Islands by 12 with the likes of Alba Redondo, 2021 Ballon d'Or winner Aléxia Putellas, Mariona Caldentey, and soon to be 2023 Ballon d'Or winner Aitana Bonmatí on the scoresheet. (Though even winning the World Cup for the Spanish players would be overshadowed by the machismo of Spanish Football Federation President Luis Rubiales and his forcing a kiss on Jennifer Hermoso during the medal ceremony. Combining that with long-term concerns over coach Jorge Vilda's treatment of the players, helps to highlight that even in the most successful of teams, the fight for respect and equality is ongoing, and far from won).

Elsewhere in Europe heavier defeats were being recorded with Georgia losing 15-0 at home to Sweden, Moldova losing 15-0 away to Switzerland, while Belgium beat Armenia 19-0, and European champions England beat Latvia 20-0 in a chastening night at the Keepmoat Stadium, Doncaster.

It was clear that the women's game needed the Nations League format every bit as much as the men's, maybe even more. And in late 2023, the inaugural UEFA Women's Nations League began. And just like the men's, it was transformative for those at the foot of the rankings.

Latvia, victims of that horrible night against England two years earlier managed three wins in their League C campaign – home and away against Andorra, and home against Moldova to finish second in their group behind Malta.

Elsewhere across the five groups in League C, matches were competitive, scorelines respectable (with the exception of the nine-nil defeat of the Faroe Islands by Montenegro in Podgorica).

Georgia, who lost by 15 to Sweden, came away with a four-two win over Luxembourg, and two draws against Lithuania in Vilnius, and against Luxembourg in Esch-Zur-Alzette.

Moldova, who lost by 15 against Switzerland drew three of their matches against Andorra nil-nil, Malta nil-nil, and Latvia with a spirited three-all draw that required two stoppage-time goals from the Latvians to deny them victory.

Indeed, of all 19 nations that competed in League C of the Nations League, only two failed to register a point. But even there, positives could be found.

The Faroe Islands proved that their nine-nil defeat to Montenegro was just a bad day at the office with a narrow one-nil loss against the same side in Tórshavn, followed up by one-nil losses, home and away, to Cyprus, a two-one defeat to Azerbaijan at home before a one-nil loss in Baku.

Armenia, who lost by 19 to Belgium, scored in all but one of their games, losing two-one and four-one to Kazakhstan, four-one and five-one to Estonia, and four-nil and six-one against group winners Israel.

Both Armenia and the Faroe Islands had been competitive, and close enough to their nearest rivals to inspire no small amount of hope for the future. Progress had been made and would be again.

For all 19 countries down in League C, the Nations League had been a positive experience where, like the men, they had been able to build confidence, express themselves, and have an attacking intent. A bridge to help build stronger results against the continents giants in the next round of qualifiers.

It had been a positive experience for all. At least all who had taken part.

Because of the 54 UEFA nations remaining after Russia's suspension, three had been missing: Liechtenstein, Gibraltar, and San Marino

Iceland men's Euro 2016 squad was chosen from just 100 professional footballers of Icelandic descent. One hundred professionals plying their trade abroad, or in the Besta deild karla – the top-flight in Icelandic football.

The Besta deild karla has existed since 1912, serving Iceland's 400,000 population with competitive football, slowly building its quality through exposure to European competition for the league and cup winners, coaching development, and a programme of indoor venues so that young talent could play all year round.

A slow and steady progress that culminated in 2016 with qualification for their first ever major tournament and that year's European Championships.

Two draws against Portugal and Hungary, followed by a two-one win over Austria saw them reach the knock-out stages, where they promptly knocked out England before losing to France in the quarter finals.

It had taken them 100 years, but Iceland had made it to the big time. A feat they would repeat two years later with a first ever appearance at the World Cup finals.

It is a story of hope for any football nation – that anything can be achieved with the right mindset, patience, determination, and will.

It is also a story that highlights that nothing can be achieved instantly. And certainly not without the basic foundations from the grassroots up.

Nations the size of Latvia, Armenia, Turkey can build women's programmes relatively quickly to serve the growing desire for women's football. Heavy defeats the inevitable result when burgeoning national teams come up against established teams with decades of experience and development behind them.

But what of Europe's micro-states? How do you create a women's national team from a population of no more than 35,000, with no established league or club system?

For Liechtenstein, Gibraltar, and San Marino, stepping into international football – even the calmer waters of the Nations League – is a daunting prospect.

There are only seven men's club sides within the 62 square miles of the Alpine principality of Liechtenstein. One too few to create a national football league – UEFA stipulate that a league must consist of no fewer than eight teams.

Of those seven clubs, only one – FC Triesen – has a women's team. Formed in 1996, they plough a lone furrow, playing in the lower reaches of the Swiss football pyramid, playing on while other teams have formed and folded around them.

When a first ever Liechtenstein Women's National Team was formed in 2019, it was FC Triesen who formed the backbone of the team – along with those who went to Switzerland to further their footballing ambitions.

Since their first official international match in 2021 – a two-one defeat to Luxembourg – they have played 12 more friendly fixtures, losing to, but being competitive against, Cyprus, Kosovo, and Andorra twice.

They have also played six matches against Gibraltar, who have also been taking those tentative first steps into international football.

Where players from Liechtenstein have an opportunity to play for nearby clubs in Switzerland, Gibraltar's women do not. They are limited to the amateur, five-team Gibraltar Women's Football League that has been running since 2016 and has been won four years running by Lions Gibraltar, with Europa finishing second behind them four years running.

Considered a development league by UEFA rather than a senior competition, Lions Gibraltar and Europa are denied the opportunity to represent Gibraltar in European club competitions.

They have, however, had the opportunity to play beyond the tiny confines of Gibraltar's 2.6 square miles in the Island Games.

Since 2011 they have lost to the likes of the Isle of Man and Greenland (nine-nil and eight-nil respectively in 2011), the Western Isles and Gotland (five-nil and three-nil in 2015), the Isle of Wight and Hitra (eight-one and one-nil in 2017), and Jersey and the Isle of Man (six-two and a much closer two-one to the team who inflicted their heaviest defeat eight years earlier in 2019).

The Gibraltar Women's National Football Team, like Liechtenstein's, played their first FIFA-sanctioned fixture in 2021, with a squad made up mostly of Lions Gibraltar and Europa players, along with a smattering of Gibraltarians studying and playing their football in England and Spain.

On 24 June 2021 they lost four-one to Liechtenstein in Ruggell, before a two-one defeat in a second match three days later.

A second head-to-head in November in Gibraltar saw the home side record their first ever win, one-nil on the 26th, before a three-two defeat on the 29th.

Slow and steady progress that has also seen them play further friendlies against Andorra, losing four-one, the Faroe Islands, losing one-nil, Hungary, where they lost by 12, and Panama, which ended in a seven-nil loss.

A third pair of games against Liechtenstein in February 2024 saw Gibraltar lose three-two on the 22nd, before a one-all draw on the 25th.

From such a small pool of players, with such a limited amount of experience, it is perhaps understandable – Liechtenstein and Gibraltar's reluctance to throw their fledgling teams into World Cup and European Championship qualifying campaigns, against European and World champions. Neither team was entered into qualification for the 2025 Euros.

But soon, with the desire of their players to represent their countries beyond a series of safe friendly matches – to truly test themselves – you can't help but feel that their sacrifice, their perseverance in the face of limited opportunity to play the game they love, taking that next step, is the very least that they deserve. Especially now with the introduction of Nations League, offering a welcome opportunity to develop and progress.

As Elia Benedettini, so passionately explained in the San Marino mission statement:

…the concerns related to the result become secondary: the passion, the will to be there at all costs and the pride of defending one's flag in the presence of the great European nations matters much more.

Liechtenstein and Gibraltar are almost there. And when they do finally make it, it will become fifty-four, minus one.

In the eighties and nineties, two women's teams from San Marino played in the Italian women's football pyramid. However, both the Dogana and Cosmos women's teams disbanded within a few years of each other before the millennium.

In 2004 the San Marino Football Federation launched a club side for women that fluctuated between the regional leagues of Serie C and D until 2017, when it was replaced by San Marino Academy.

Under this new guise, the team gained promotion to Serie B in 2019 and finished third behind Lazio in a Covid-truncated season the year after. One season in Serie A followed, but San Marino Academy finished 11th and were relegated back into Serie B, where they remain. And while this success is impressive, it was born out of a squad mostly made up of Italian women.

The team of 2022 only had five Sammarinese among its ranks, two of whom were goalkeepers. But by the summer of 2024 that number was down to two and would soon be one with the retirement of captain Yesica Soledad Menin.

With that, Magda Nicolini became the only Sammarinese playing senior women's football in the republic. Another, Eleonara Cecchini, who had played in that Serie A season facing down the likes of Juventus, Inter Milan, AC Milan, Fiorentina, Roma, and Napoli, moved to Canada, where she plays third tier football for St Catherine's Roma Wolves.

After nearly 20 years of a San Marino representative side in Italian football, two senior Sammarinese players seemed scant reward. Something needed to change.

Football is nothing without grassroots. Without a pathway for players to progress along.

And, albeit late to the game, San Marino Academy created that pathway, with under 12, under 15, and under 17 sides to enable girls to play. Though, with that leap up to a senior team littered with seasoned Italian players, there have been only a handful progress.

Another approach was needed. Which came in April 2024. And finally, a first-ever, female San Marino national team.

Held in San Marino, the Under-16 UEFA Development Tournament featured national teams from San Marino, Georgia, Estonia, and Luxembourg.

San Marino u16s (Photo courtesy of San Marino FA)

And on 16 April, a first ever competitive game for a female Sammarinese national team took place against a side of young Georgian players, themselves hoping that the experience would be a stepping stone up into the Georgian senior side. Helping to improve on bruising scores suffered by their current crop of national team players.

Despite losing seven-four (Giulia Penserini cancelled out an early Georgian goal, before Khelashvili made it two-one at half time) San Marino had discovered something they had never possessed before in international football – a prolific goal scorer.

Eliza Terenzi, just turned 16, became the first ever Sammarinese to score an international hat-trick with goals in the 65th, 66th, and 94th minute. Wheeling away with her arm raised, finger pointing to the sky, rushing towards her team-mates to celebrate, Terenzi would be the revelation of the tournament for San Marino. Because she hadn't finished scoring.

Goals in the 2nd and 31st minutes against Luxembourg showed she had what it took at international level. A six-two defeat again showing that, as a team, a lack of experience, a lack of opportunity at this level hadn't created a chasm. Passion, endeavour, and burgeoning talent had seen San Marino compete against nations with more established women's programmes, complete with senior national teams.

Solid performances, wonderful exposure, and the revelation of a goalscoring talent may have been enough for some at a first-ever international tournament, but not this young San Marino team.

San Marino v Estonia (Photo courtesy of San Marino FA)

Against Estonia, Elisa Terenzi had a goal disallowed for offside on ten minutes, had hit the post after 16, and had a free kick brilliantly saved by Regina Ivanona in the Estonian goal on 20 minutes.

But it would be team-mate Anna Benedettini who would open the scoring on 48 minutes, giving San Marino a first-ever lead to try and hold, which they did until the 91st minute, when Estonia equalised right at the death.

Despite that disappointment, San Marino saw out the penalty shoot-out with a calmness and composure unbefitting their years and experience: Anna Benedettini, Asya Yazici, Elisa Terenzi, Greta Paone, and goalkeeper Arianna Forcellini scoring all five, while Hanna Haavitsu saw her fifth and final penalty for Estonia crash back off the crossbar.

And with that, and in only their second competitive game, San Marino had won.

Testament to the idea if you give someone an opportunity, let their potential free, amazing things can happen. Amazing things in women's football in San Marino.

Penalty shoot out celebration (Photo courtesy of San Marino FA)

It was an optimism shared by the football federation themselves who celebrated in:

'…the common intent to promote and inspire the dreams of the young girls from San Marino in the practice of the most beautiful game in the world

and wearing the most prestigious and romantic jersey of all: the one that represents their country.

The development tournament that took place here last week has made history for San Marino football, with the first whistle of the first match.

Bit, it also gave – speaking of strong emotions mentioned above – the first, well-deserved victory, which came at the end of the game against Estonia – played by the girls with great application for the entire 90 minutes, with the ability to overcome critical moments until reaching the final jubilation. Jubilation appropriately emphasized by a grandstand full of girls from the youth section, that throughout the duration of the tournament were warm, colourful, tireless.'

The mantra that "if you can see it, you can be it," sowing the seeds for a bright future in women's football in San Marino.

It may take a little time, but if Eleonara Cecchini and Magda Nicolini can remain patient for a little while longer, they may yet get to taste international football in a first ever senior Sammarinese women's national team before their careers are over. Because the under 16's are coming.

And behind them – a grandstand of warm, colourful, tireless, and even younger Sammarinese football hopefuls.

The women's game in the Most Serene Republic may be behind even the likes of Liechtenstein and Gibraltar, but the foundations are now in place. Players are developing, with the opportunity to represent their country now an even greater motivating factor.

Given the passion and desire that has always been there, all the way back in those early teams of Dogana and Cosmos, and now among this new crop of young players, combine that with this new opportunity to shine in a new national team, and who would bet against them taking their passion and making it all the way to a first ever

Elisa Terenzi (Photo courtesy of San Marino FA)

senior women's team, the Nations League, European and World Cup qualifying?

Filling the entire roster of UEFA nations with a women's team for the first time.

It may not happen for years, maybe not in time for the next cycle of World Cup qualifying and the next round of the Nations League, but this new groundswell of talent means that, surely, it must. And when it does, it will be an important moment, a statement of validation, for women's football not only in the shadow of Monte Titano, but for women's football across Europe, and far beyond.

And when it happens – Elisa Terenzi – remember the name.

Line-ups: 28.04.24, Stadio Fonte dell'Ovo, Acquaviva

San Marino

1 Arianna Forcellini
3 Anna Benedettini © (1)
4 Cristina Carli
5 Elisa Paolini
6 Mikaela Tamagnini (Anita Bianchi 55') (Teresa Ragazzini 87')
7 Giulia Penserini (Silvia Bonciucci 87')
8 Asya Yazici
9 Greta Paone
10 Elisa Terenzi
11 Vanessa Zanotti (Alessia Moroni 51')
13 Sofia Stifani (Alice Maresi 87')

Estonia

12 Regina Ivanona
3 Reti Marleen Ränk
5 Sofia Priideman (Säde Sepp 46')
8 Maribel Laidmets (Adele Sofia Berg 46')
9 Mia Martina Kaalman ©
10 Renate Väli (Arina Uzjukina 46')
11 Hanna Veensalu
14 Gerda-Liise Pärnik (Mirell Luik 46')
18 Gerda Liisa Matson
19 Meele Kelder (Rianna Väärsi 46')
20 Jelizaveta Južaninova

Under-16 UEFA Development Tournament

16.04.24 – Estonia 2 Luxembourg 3
16.04.24 – San Marino 4 Georgia 7
18.04.24 – Luxembourg 1 Georgia 4
18.04.24 – San Marino 1 Estonia 1
21.04.24 – Luxembourg 6 San Marino 2
21.04.24 – Georgia 5 Estonia 2

	P	W	D	L	F	A	Pts
Georgia	3	3	0	0	16	7	9
Luxembourg	3	2	0	1	10	8	6
San Marino	3	0	1	2	7	14	2
Estonia	3	0	1	2	5	9	1

Chapter Six – Islands in the Stream

A GOOD IDEA travels well. Transcending vast distances. Cutting through disparate cultures and beliefs. A good idea is a good idea no matter which way you look at the world, or frame what is going on around it.

In 2019, one year after the inaugural Nations League season in Europe, CONCACAF – the Confederation of North, Central America and Caribbean Association Football began their own Nations League journey.

With an even broader church of opportunity and ability within its members than UEFA, the CONCACAF Nations League has provided an avenue to develop football across its congregation. A congregation that features perennial World Cup Finals participants and regional giants in Mexico, USA, and Costa Rica, sometime qualifiers in Panama, Honduras, El Salvador, Canada, Trinidad & Tobago, and Jamaica, and the rest. The rest consisting largely of island states of various sizes whose national teams – pre-Nations League – used to play relatively sparingly in CONCACAF Gold Cup qualifiers and World Cup qualifiers, often with the potential of years between fixtures.

CONCACAF Gold Cup 2019 Guyana v Panama (Flickr by EDrost88 (Erik Drost) cc-by-2.0)

Throw into the mix four members who don't have FIFA membership due to their affiliation with the French and Dutch football federations

(Saint Martin and Guadeloupe being members of the French Football Federation, Bonaire and Sint Maarten affiliated to the Royal Dutch Football Association) and their opportunity to play is reduced to potentially a solitary pair of qualifying fixtures every two years in the CONCACAF Gold Cup.

Under such conditions it was no surprise that some football associations struggled to maintain active national teams, let alone allow them, and those who aspired to be a part of them, to develop and thrive.

And so, in 2019, CONCACAF introduced the Nations League, split across three divisions based on ability. With four or six fixtures played across a three-month period from September to November 2019, smaller CONCACAF members found themselves with the opportunity to play as many times as they sometimes did in a four-year-cycle.

The results were profound, spiritually if not statistically, and created the building blocks for near-dormant footballing communities to spring back into life.

The US Virgin Islands, population 87,000, situated in the Leeward Islands east of Puerto Rico, have been anchored near the foot of the FIFA World Rankings (at the time of writing 208th out of 210) since the first FIFA affiliated US Virgin Islands national team was formed in 1992. Playing regularly for the first time in their history, they came last in their group containing the champions Barbados, who beat them one-nil and four-nil, the Cayman Islands, who won two-nil and one-nil, and non-FIFA Saint Martin, where the US Virgin Islands claimed a precious win (Aaron Dennis, a journeyman through the lower leagues of America with the Long Island Rough Riders, Ocean City Nor'easters, Arizona United, Penn FC, and a reformed New York Cosmos with his countries first ever Nations League goal in a two-one victory).

Saint Martin, who would finish on nine points after wins against all three teams in their group, would take their revenge in the last round of games – Yannick Bellechasse, whose career has taken him from Junior Stars FC in Saint Martin to Flames United in neighbouring Sint Maarten, and Lymers FC in Anguilla, scoring the winner.

The second Nations League – held a year late in 2022 due to Covid-19 – saw the US Virgin Islands claim four points in a series of six closely fought League C games – drawing with eventual winner Sint Maarten one-all and beating the Turks and Caicos Islands three-two.

In 2023 they managed one point in a draw with the Cayman Islands, before narrow defeats to winners Aruba, the Cayman Islands winning the return fixture two-one in front of 647 spectators at the Truman Bodden Sports Complex in George Town.

Sixteen games in four years. Two wins, two draws, 12 defeats. It may not seem like a decent return, but for a team starved of opportunity, it represents so much more than cold statistics. It is a pathway for players to develop, in a competition in which they can be competitive. A tournament that helps forge a sporting identity, a pride in representing, supporting, your country. Sometimes the result of a match can exceed a simple scoreline.

The effect the Nations League has had on the US Virgin Islands in providing more opportunity, in instilling a greater pride in their national team has been reflected across the region. Small islands have active national teams to support. Young players have a goal to achieve now, a clear pathway into international football, and with it, the pride of representing your country.

And while many of the US Virgin Islands fellow members of the FIFA World Rankings 200 club haven't seen transformative change in their fortunes, they have mostly been competitive, and progress can be measured.

The US Virgin islands near neighbours in the Leeward Islands, the British Virgin Islands (population 28,000, currently ranked 207th out of 210 by FIFA, who joined football's governing body in 1974) finished last in their group in the first two editions of the Nations League, losing all four matches in 2019, drawing two and losing two in 2022, but in 2023 they claimed their first win (three-one against Turks and Caicos Islands) along with a one-all draw with eventual winners Dominica.

The Turks and Caicos Islands (located in the northern West Indies, population 47,000, joined FIFA in 1998, ranked 206th in the world) won two matches in 2019, three in 2022, and despite managing just one draw in 2023, played out three narrow defeats. For the first time in their history, a little disappointment could steel them for their 2024 campaign.

While many of the FIFA 200 club have held their own, one has thrived in the Nations League.

The Bahamas, equidistant between the Florida Keys and Cuba, ranked 200th in the world, won promotion at the first time of asking in the Nations League. Three wins and a draw in a group with Bonaire and the British Virgin Islands saw them promoted into a daunting League B group in 2022 with Nicaragua, Trinidad and Tobago, and Saint Vincent and the Grenadines.

They were not over-awed and finished third, beating Saint Vincent and the Grenadines at home one-nil, before drawing one-all away. One-nil and three-nil defeats to Trinidad and Tobago, and a two-nil loss at home to

Nicaragua, followed by a four-nil defeat at the 20,000 capacity Estadio Nacional de Fútbol in Managua, rounded off an unbelievable campaign, playing teams far above their supposed level.

In 2023 they had a tougher time of it against Guyana (who, despite coming from the continent of South America, play in CONCACAF with fellow South American compatriots Suriname and French Guiana), Puerto Rico, and Antigua and Barbuda.

A narrow three-two defeat to the eventual champions Guyana, and a two-all draw away to Antigua and Barbuda was the high-water mark for the Bahamas, while two six-one defeats home and away to Puerto Rico helped to underline the quality among mid-ranking CONCACAF members.

Relegation back to League C was confirmed when their final group game couldn't be fulfilled due to severe storms that raged for days. With no end in sight, CONCACAF cancelled the fixture, and with it went any chance of salvation from the drop.

Next time out, back in league C, it will be Barbados and the US Virgin Islands for the Bahamas. And, possibly for the first time ever, steeled by those competitive League B performances, excitement and anticipation for these national team fixtures will be laced with a genuine sense of expectation.

Something almost inconceivable before the Nations League.

The Nations League has had a transformative effect on those Caribbean football nations near the foot of the FIFA rankings. Concentrated, regular fixtures have not only rejuvenated football on the pitch, but also pride and passion off it. Competitive, closely fought matches helping communities to celebrate their identity, their home. *Their* team, their country, proudly standing shoulder to shoulder with sporting peers. Victories over local rivals a welcome, and, given the paucity of fixtures pre-Nations League, sometimes unique experience.

But if the effect has been transformative for the Caribbean's members of the FIFA 200-club, then it has been seismic for those on the outside looking in.

For Saint Martin, Sint Maarten (the Dutch half of the same island – Saint Martin being French), Guadeloupe (a French overseas department), and Bonaire (a Public Body of the Netherlands), international football before the Nations League came even more sparingly than for their neighbours.

Without FIFA affiliation, they have been unable to take part in the World Cup qualifiers every four years, leaving CONCACAF Gold Cup qualifying every two years as their only international outlet.

But in the Nations League, national identity and sporting pride have been let loose, and every nation, no matter the size, has taken the opportunity with both hands.

The 34 square-mile Saint Martin, population 73,000, situated 190 miles east of Puerto Rico, began Nations League life in 2019 with three wins and three defeats, finishing third in a group with Barbados, the Cayman Islands, and the US Virgin Islands. Thirty-seven-year-old Wilfried Dalmat, who in his earlier career won the French League 1 title with Nantes, and the Belgian First Division with Standard Liège scoring Saint Martin's first Nations League goal in a two-one defeat to the US Virgin Islands.

In 2022 they came bottom of a tough three-team group with Saint Kitts and Nevis and Aruba, drawing at home to Aruba, and away to Saint Kitts and Nevis.

But better was to come in 2023, when they topped the group over Bonaire and Anguilla, conceding just the one goal to gain promotion to League B.

Regular football creating something that had come only sparingly before – national pride in their team.

Across the island, the 42,000 strong Sint Maarten had a tougher start to their Nations League career. Heavy defeats to Guadeloupe and the Turks and Caicos Islands (five-one and five-two respectively) in their opening 2019 fixtures were followed up by better showings in the return matches, losing two-one to Guadeloupe, and three-two away to the Turks and Caicos Islands. Gerwin Darrell Miguel "Smally" Lake, winger for Sportvereniging Poortugaal in the Dutch fifth tier, scored five of Sint Maarten's six goals as they finished bottom of the group.

Much better was to come in 2022 when Sint Maarten topped the group over Bonaire, the Turks and Caicos Islands and the US Virgin Islands. Gerwin "Smally" Lake starring again with a four-goal haul in an eight-two win over the Turks and Caicos Islands, and a hat trick in a six-one victory over Bonaire.

In 2023 they held their own in League B, coming third in a group containing Guadeloupe, Saint Lucia, and Saint Kitts and Nevis. Their two wins from their six matches came in a one-nil away win over Saint Kitts and Nevis (the winner coming from Ilounga Pata, who plays his football for Sheriff Tiraspol in the unrecognised breakaway state of Transnistria in Moldova) and a two-one victory in Saint Lucia. "Smally" Lake scoring the winner in the 58th minute, after an opening goal from Chovanie Amatkarijo who plays for Östersunds FK in the Swedish second tier, to avenge an opening day five-one defeat.

Bonaire, a 111 square-mile island, 50 miles north of the Venezuelan coast, has been the picture of consistency across their three Nations League campaigns. Despite a population of just 24,000, they have finished second every time, behind the Bahamas in 2019, Sint Maarten in 2022, and Saint Martin in 2023.

In that time, they have chalked up seven wins, two draws, and five defeats, and their second-place finish in 2023 saw them promoted into League B for the 2024 campaign, where they will come up against El Salvador, Montserrat and Saint Vincent and the Grenadines. No mean feat for a nation of that size.

All the non-FIFA Caribbean nations have benefitted enormously from the Nations League experience. The opportunity to play regularly, bringing nations together, inspiring them in a way only sport can. But of all four, one nation stands out in what it has achieved.

Guadeloupe's 380,000 population is similar in size to that of Iceland. And like Iceland, their national team has been punching well above its weight. Especially given the lack of opportunity afforded it.

Located south of Antigua and Barbuda, and north of Dominica, Guadeloupe won four from four in their 2019 League C campaign, conceding only two goals in the process. Home form was especially impressive with thumping five-one and ten-nil victories over Sint Maarten and the Turks and Caicos Islands respectively.

2022 saw a solid League B season for Guadeloupe, who finished second behind Cuba – Guadeloupe being the only team to inflict a defeat on them. Two wins over Barbados was enough to see them pip Antigua and Barbuda to second spot.

Then, in 2023, Guadeloupe won their League B group with five wins from six against Saint Lucia, Sint Maarten, and Saint Kitts and Nevis.

Ange-Freddy Plumain scored five goals across the six matches to round off what had been a turbulent time for the winger. Signing for Rukh Lviv in the Ukrainian Premier League in 2022, he soon found himself in a war zone. And with the league suspended for a time as Ukraine battled to defend itself against Russian aggression, Plumain went out on loan in Israel, first to Hapoel Tel Aviv for the remainder of the 2021/2022 season, then Sektzia Ness Ziona for the first half of the 22/23 season, and Bnei Sakhnin for the second.

He finally made his Rukh Lviv debut at the start of the 23/24 season in a Ukrainian Premier League still affected by the war, with displaced clubs playing far from home, and matches played behind closed doors if safety dictated.

Playing in the Caribbean and scoring goals for your national team must have been a welcome release from such a situation, and a source of tremendous pride – as witnessed in the distances needed to travel to represent Guadeloupe.

He isn't alone in that regard.

Taïryk Arconte scored three goals in Guadeloupe's 2023 Nations League season, coming from French Ligue 2 side Pau. Matthias Phaëton also scored three, between playing for CSKA Sofia in Bulgaria. Luther Archimède travelled from California where he plays for Monterrey Bay in the second tier, Jérôme Roussillon from Union Berlin in the Bundesliga.

Even players based in Guadeloupe travel vast distances to represent their country – their love and passion for Guadeloupean football inspiring them to go as far as they can each season in the Coupe de France.

The Coupe de France is to French club football what the FA Cup is to their English counterparts. Its prestige undimmed, it is open to all amateur and professional sides in the country, as well as to teams in the overseas departments and territories – from Tahiti and New Caledonia in Polynesia, to Mayotte in the Indian Ocean, Saint Pierre and Miquelon in the North Atlantic to France's Caribbean dependencies.

It was CS Moulien of Guadeloupe who became the first ever overseas club to compete in the Coupe de France, making the 8,500-mile round-trip to play FC Dieppe in 1961, losing three-two.

In 1980 they travelled again, this time beating Blois Football 41 two-one (to be the first side from Guadeloupe to win on the French mainland) before losing in the round of 64 at home to CS Thonon. Then in 2006 they lost after extra time, away to Clermont Foot two-one, and to CSO Amnéville in 2010 two-nil, FC Mulhouse in 2016 three-nil, SAS Épinal in 2017 six-two, and finally, away to SO Romorantin in 2023, this time losing four-nil.

Despite being the first, they are far from the only team from Guadeloupe to represent their country on the French mainland.

ASG Juventus followed them in 1964, and since then AS Cygne Noir, AS Red Star de Pointe-à-Pitre, L'Etoile de Morne-à-l'Eau, US Baie Manhault (who went all that way in 1998 to lose 12-1 to Dijon FCO), Evolucas, ASC Siroco des Abymes, Phare du Canal, and JS Vieux-Habitants have made the trip. But it is only L'Etoile de Morne-à-l'Eau who have come back with a second win for Guadeloupe, beating AS Muret one-nil in 2000.

The passion and pride in representing Guadeloupe clearly transcends distance, and, often in the past, the limited opportunity to do so. But the Nations League has enabled a footballing community to flourish, resulting in a 2024 Nations League season that will be spent for the first time in League A, where Guadeloupe will come up against Costa Rica and Guatemala.

And given where they have come from, and how far they have gone (and are prepared to go) it would be no huge surprise if they didn't flourish among such lofty CONCACAF opposition.

Like its European cousin, the CONCACAF Nations League has proven to be a near universal success. The extra games, and the regularity of them, helping to create a positive environment in which football can flourish. Near dormant teams are playing consistently, inspiring the next generation and fans alike. Pride in their team, a precious thing, now that they can be seen and savoured. And with the tiered groups, positive results, goals, wins – things rarely experienced before, or too far and few across too much time – football fans have something to believe in. And with that belief – hope. Of more wins, or even becoming champions, promotion, welcoming some of the local football giants to your shores.

It has been a near universal success. But not complete. As with UEFA and San Marino, for one CONCACAF nation, the wins haven't come.

And like San Marino, victories, successes, need to be measured using other metrics. Metrics above and beyond the statistics of league tables and scorelines. Those little fables that have sustained the Sammarinese, they are also needed elsewhere.

There is only one country in FIFA with a smaller population than Anguilla, whose 15,752 inhabitants dwarf that of Caribbean neighbours Montserrat, it's 4,488 islanders, and their more successful national football team.

But, as always, statistics only tell a fraction of the story.

Because Montserrat's population never used to be this small.

Another of the Leeward Islands' chain, Montserrat's nearest neighbours include Guadeloupe, Antigua, and Nevis.

An otherwise tiny, relatively anonymous speck on a globe, it became famous, or infamous, in 1995 when the Soufrière Hills volcano erupted, causing catastrophic devastation. The capital, Plymouth, along with the entire southern half of the island was destroyed beneath pyroclastic flows. Nineteen people died, and two-thirds of the island's population had to flee their homes and the island itself.

To this day, the southern half of the island remains uninhabitable, and Brades – the largest settlement in the north – has replaced Plymouth as Montserrat's unofficial capital.

Among it all, football endured.

In 2002, a new national stadium was built in the north of the island (one of its tenants being possibly the most important football team on all of Montserrat – Montserrat Volcano Observatory Tremors FC), and the country went about rebuilding the national team as well as the rest of the island's infrastructure.

Brades, Montserrat (creative commons by 2.0 - flickr.com: davidstanleytravel)

In the summer of 2002 Montserrat, second last in the FIFA rankings at the time, travelled to the Himalayas and Bhutan – the last placed team – to play "The Other Final," a match concocted by some disaffected Dutch supporters, whose national team had failed to qualify for the World Cup Finals. Played on the same day as the World Cup Final itself, the film documenting such a remarkable game helped shine a light on the passion, joy, and importance of the Bhutanese and Montserratian teams, despite their lowly position in world football.

And from there, and utilising the now widespread Montserratian diaspora, they set about building a national football team to be proud of.

The hard work paid off.

By the time of the first CONCACAF Nations League started in 2019, Montserrat had raised themselves up high enough to be placed in League B, where they won two, drew two, and lost two of their six matches against El Salvador, Dominican Republic, and Saint Lucia, finishing second in Group B.

Their Nations League squads regularly feature the likes of Brandon Comley, who played one English Premier League match for Queens Park Rangers in the 2014/15 season, before a long career in League Two with

Carlisle United, Grimsby Town, Colchester United, and Walsall, and Jeriel Dorsett who has played in the Scottish Premiership with Kilmarnock, and in League One and Two in England with Reading and Rochdale respectively.

And for the last ten years Montserrat's squads have also included one of the most accomplished and successful players in its national team's history – Lyle Taylor,

Since his international debut in 2015, London-born Taylor has juggled playing for the nation he qualifies to represent through his grandparents (initially in sporadic World Cup and CONCACAF Gold Cup qualifying fixtures, and latterly in the Nations League) while also playing at a very high level in club football.

Since his debut in League One with AFC Bournemouth in 2010, Taylor has gone on to play more than 500 professional games, scoring 170 goals across the leagues in England and Scotland. From Hereford United, AFC Wimbledon and his latest club Colchester United in League Two, to Sheffield United, Scunthorpe United, Wycombe Wanderers, and Cambridge United in League One, and Charlton Athletic, Nottingham Forest, and Birmingham City in the English Championship. He also had a prolific spell in the Scottish Championship with Falkirk, scoring 29 goals in 42 appearances.

And while he never got to play in the English Premier League like his international teammate Brandom Comley, who made a single appearance for QPR, he did make the Premier League in Scotland with Partick Thistle. His 36 appearances and 11 goals took him to some of football's most iconic grounds and teams: Celtic's Celtic Park, Easter Road, the home of Hibernian, Hearts' Tynecastle and Aberdeen's Pittodrie.
He won the League Two play offs in 2016 with AFC Wimbledon, the League One play offs with Charlton Athletic in 2019, and the Championship play off in 2022 with Nottingham Forest.

And while his club career was taking off, Lyle Taylor still made sure he was available for the nation of his grandparents. The honour of representing his heritage worth the long string of connecting flights and missed club games (Leagues One and Two continuing through international windows) for qualifying fixtures that would make few waves outside the Montserratian diaspora.

His debut in March 2015 against Curaçao in the Ergilio Hato Stadium, Willemstad in a 2018 World Cup qualifier ended in a two-one defeat. Though it would only take him 24 minutes of international football for him to register his first international goal.

To date he remains Montserrat's highest international goal scorer with 13 from 20 appearances, including a prolific six in five matches in 2021 against Antigua & Barbuda, El Salvador, and Grenada in qualifying fixtures for the World Cup in 2022, and a goal against Trinidad & Tobago in Gold Cup qualifying.

The only thing missing from his international CV is a goal on Montserratian soil – all 13 of his international strikes have come away from the Blakes Estate Stadium, the 1,000-seat capacity home pitch that replaced the old national stadium lost – along with the rest of the old capital Plymouth – when the Soufrière Hills volcano erupted in 1995.

There is still time, and now with the Nations League, there is more opportunity. It is the least the pride in his country, and the lengths and sacrifices he has made to represent them deserves.

For in Lyle Taylor, like those players of every lower-ranked nation on the international stage, we have the very essence of what it means to represent your people, your country. The importance it holds, the honour it bestows, the pride and passion in pulling on that national team shirt as great as any play-off victory at Wembley Stadium.

No matter the lengths it takes, and the relative obscurity all that effort generates in the grand scheme of world football.

With such talent and dedication to the national cause as Taylor, Comley, and Dorsett, Montserrat have comfortably held their own in League B, winning three of their six games in 2023 against Nicaragua, Dominican Republic, and Barbados.

In the next instalment they go again against El Salvador, Saint Vincent and the Grenadines, and Bonaire.

From out of the literal ashes of their devastated country, Montserrat have risen higher in footballing circles than they have ever been. The misfortune of a devastating volcano producing sporting opportunities for the sons of the displaced in professional football clubs in England and beyond.

The price – 19 dead, more than half an island lost, two thirds displaced around the world – is too much. But the national pride in a team doing well, representing Montserrat, must do wonders to keep this scattered community together.

Montserrat have long since left the basement of the FIFA World Rankings, seemingly never to return. A slow and steady 20-year march, up and away.

Up and away from their fellow Caribbean minnows, Anguilla.

Anguilla is a 35 square mile island, east of Puerto Rico and the Virgin Islands. Taking Montserrat out of the equation, it vies with the Polynesian Cook Islands in Oceania as the smallest FIFA nation – both populations fluctuating in and around 15,000. Some years Anguilla is smaller, some years the Cook Islands. For that reason, both national football teams struggle to make an impact.

Since its first international match in 1985 (a one-nil defeat by the British Virgin Islands in a Leeward Islands tournament) Anguilla have only ever won two competitive football matches. In February 2001 they beat a yet-to-recover Montserrat four-one in Caribbean Cup qualification. They then beat Saint Martin two-one in 2010 in the same qualifying competition.

Since 1985 there have been six friendly-match wins, three apiece against Saint Martin and the British Virgin Islands, the last coming in February 2022 with a two-one win at the Stade Thelbert Carti in Quartier-d'Orleans, Saint Martin.

In between Anguilla's successes have come crushing defeats: 13-0 to Panama in World Cup qualifying in 2021, a 15-0 friendly defeat to Trinidad and Tobago in 2019, 10-0 to Nicaragua in the same year (the third defeat by 10 in their history). They have also lost by 14 to Grenada and Guyana, and by 12 to El Salvador.

No great surprise given the tiny population to choose a national team from, and the paucity of opportunity, even when a team has been selected.

In the 34 years from their first match in 1985 to the start of the first CONCACAF Nations League in 2019, Anguilla played just 68 national team matches – roughly two a year, though sometimes they went years without a single game.

No surprise then that coming up against footballing giants of the confederation, sides that have qualified for World Cup finals and who play more than double the matches than the regions minnows, that heavy defeats are the outcome.

For decades that was your lot if you were the likes of Anguilla – intermittent, often unequal matches. The odd friendly against a local fellow-minnow nation. Then nothing, for two years.

But, in 2019, came the good idea, and 24 matches in less than six years.

There can be no FIFA ranking for pride, passion, the sense of meaning and identity that a national football team can provide a community. That feeling of togetherness, that celebration of culture, of roots centuries deep. Of friendships, camaraderie, of those who have gone before us, who inspired, passed down that passion.

One might think that you could rank nations – the fervour of the Argentinians, Brazilians, Italians coming out above others – but you cannot.

Different cultures do things differently, but the result is no different – that almost primal, spine-tingling electricity at belonging, being a part of something. Something wonderful, handed down from those you revere. All encapsulated in your national football team. You rank that and you would have a 210-way dead-heat.

And the Nations League understands that. Feeds that. Gives opportunity for that pride and passion to flourish. For football to flourish – in whatever way each community can. Even tiny communities like Anguilla.

And despite tangible results not going their way, just like San Marino, the Nations League has given Anguilla a platform to express itself. And for a national team to coalesce, develop, improve – even if only through Sammarinese fables.

In 2019 Anguilla were in a horrible League C group with Guatemala and Puerto Rico. Four games, four defeats, including a 10-0 thumping in Guatemala City, resulted in a minus 19-goal difference. Anguilla's only goals in that 2019 season came in a three-two home defeat to Puerto Rico – Kyle Lake-Bryan scoring his nations first ever Nations League goal.

Where Montserrat could call upon English Championship strikers and other professionals, Anguilla's goal came from a player turning out for Spartans Youth in the Combined Counties League Division One – a full 10 divisions lower in the English football pyramid from Montserratian Brandon Comley's Premier League debut for QPR.

Alongside his brother Kieran (also playing for Spartans Youth), a few other Anguillan's playing in England for Flackwell Heath and Egham Town, and a squad of home-based players representing the likes of Doc's United, Diamond, Uprising, and Roaring Lions in the Anguillan Football League, Kyle Lake-Bryan travelled far and wide to represent his homeland, sacrificing much.

Pride overcoming double-digit defeats, with little fables created in the 76th minute of a match in which he was already three-nil down. October 15th, 2019 – the day he scored an international goal in front of his home fans.

For Anguilla, better was to come in 2022 when, despite finishing bottom of their group, they claimed their first ever Nations League points with a pair of draws against Dominica: nil-nil at home, and one-all away, where Jonathan Guishard's first, and, so far, only international goal shared the spoils.

Two-nil and two-one defeats to Saint Lucia rounded out the group.

The 2023 Nations League was a tougher experience for Anguilla, where despite competitive defeats home and away to Bonaire (two-nil and three-nil respectively), they were outgunned by Saint Martin – a team they traditionally did well against – losing six-nil at home and eight-nil away. The cold hard stats of the Group A table registering no goals scored, 19 conceded.

In preparation for the 2024 Nations League season, where Anguilla were drawn in the same group as Belize and the Turks and Caicos Islands, they drew one-all in a friendly with Sint Maarten, then drew nil-nil at home and one-all away to the British Virgin Islands in their FIFA World Cup 2026 qualification round. Luke Paris, defender for Uxbridge in the Isthmian League South Central Division in England, scoring the all-important goal that took the fixture to penalties. The British Virgin Islands prevailing four-three, denying Anguilla a first ever World Cup qualifying victory. Another fable of endeavour, heartbreak, but ultimately encouragement for the Caribbean minnows.

A fourth game, and well-needed goalless draw with Saint Martin, helped exorcise some of the previous season's Nations League demons in readiness for the next. The regular game time inspiring a nation, both off and on the pitch. Off it, the pride of national identity, of celebrating your homeland, supporting your national team, has galvanised the island's football fans. On it, new generations are being inspired to take up the challenge. The honour of representing your country on the international stage, as seen in these national team players facing down greater footballing nations with grit and grace, has inspired others.

Anguilla now has a flourishing boys and girls youth set-up. The Anguilla boys under-14s took part in the Caribbean Football Unions Challenge Series in the Summer of 2024, beating the Turks and Caicos Islands three-one, the US Virgin Islands five-nil, drawing with Dominica nil-nil, and the British Virgin Islands three-nil.

At the same time, in the CONCACAF under-15 girls tournament, Anguilla beat Aruba three-nil, drew against Guyana nil-nil, and narrowly lost one-nil to Bonaire and Guadeloupe.

Elsewhere, the senior Women's team prepared for their 2023 CONCACAF Women's Gold Cup qualifying league with a seven-nil friendly win over Sint Maarten, followed by a three-nil win over Saint Kitts and Nevis.

In the Gold Cup they beat the Cayman Islands three-one at home, and drew two-all away in George Town, before losing to Curaçao five-two in Willemstad, and five-one in the home leg.

They say: "if you can see it, you can be it," and the rejuvenation of the Anguilla men's national team through regular competitive Nations League football has certainly helped inspire the younger generation to take up the challenge. The pathway to regular national team football, and the challenge of taking on your rivals, representing your country will sustain Anguillan football in the years to come.

Based on the youth team results, it may even generate more positive outcomes, and that illusive first ever World Cup qualifying win, that first Nations League victory. A happy by-product from such pride and joy in celebrating your country, out there on the football pitch.

And if victory doesn't come there, then maybe it might come from a most unlikely source, and an unforeseen consequence of Nations League footballs success on both sides of the Atlantic.

Maybe victory will come via their Nations League cousins in Europe…

Line-ups: 18.11.23, Raymond E. Guishard Technical Centre, The Valley

Anguilla

1 Jelanie Lawrence ©
16 Delani Francis
5 Alexander Fleming (Keante Brooks 89')
20 Kieron Lake-Bryan
2 Kion Lee
10 Jalen Smeins
8 Jordans Deans (Jaheim Thompson 63')
12 Jonathan Guishard
9 Mekhi Connor (Dalek Moore 72')
22 Kyle Lake-Bryan (Jared Smeins 63')
13 Jauron Gayle

Bonaire

12 Denyor Cicilia
13 Mairon Serberie
18 Adri Serberie
3 Marschelon Pourier ©
20 Raemian Janga (Dangemir Cicilia 57')
15 Ginel Ronde (Jurven Koffy 46')
8 Berry Sonnenschein
9 Fabio Hierck (Christopher Isenia 46')
10 Jort Van Der Sande
19 Jonathan Libania (Fraedyen Michiel (1) 65')
17 Thierry Anthony (2) (Deyon Martijn 79')

CONCACAF Nations League, League C, Group A

07.09.23 – Anguilla 0 Saint Martin 6
11.09.23 – Saint Martin 2 Bonaire 1
12.10.23 – Bonaire 2 Anguilla 0
16.10.23 – Saint Martin 8 Anguilla 0
18.11.23 – Anguilla 0 Bonaire 3
21.11.23 – Bonaire 0 Saint Martin 4

	P	W	D	L	F	A	Pts
Saint Martin	4	4	0	0	20	1	12
Bonaire	4	2	0	2	6	6	6
Anguilla	4	0	0	4	0	19	0

Chapter Seven – San Marino v Liechtenstein
September 5, 2024

NECESSITY IS THE mother of invention. And despite the pride and passion in representing or supporting your national team, despite more closely fought matches in the Nations League that have instilled a genuine sense of progression and hope among the minnow nations of UEFA and CONCACAF, to those few who have not yet tasted victory – and, often, victory at a hitherto unprecedented regularity – there is that necessity, that last barrier to break down.

Because, after all, sportspeople want to be winners. Want to win for themselves, for their country. Elevating mini-fables into unequivocal, undisputable successes. Statistical fact. Checks in the win columns of league tables.

You don't commit to the countless hours of training, across countless days, months, years, if you are not driven by one thing above all else – to do your very best, and for that very best, at the very least every now and then, to translate into victory.

And for all bar two nations, since the inception of the Nations League in 2018 to the lead up to the 2024 edition: San Marino and Anguilla, that hard work *has* yielded cold, hard, statistical success.

Only these two have yet to break through that final barrier, and experience the euphoria, the groundswell of confidence and belief that has come for other minnow nations of experiencing international victory. Because success often breeds more success. If only you can break through that one, elusive, 90-minute barrier. And become a winner in international football.

Though it can seem almost impossible.

While others have broken through, in Europe, San Marino have not. Their nearest rivals seemingly pulling away from them with positive results in the Nations League – defeats turning into draws, draws into wins. Watching that boost driving them on, and wondering what it could do for them, if only they could get that one result.

Necessity is the mother of invention, and in trying to break through, San Marino have been very inventive, and quite possibly groundbreaking. Not only for them, but for fellow members of the FIFA rankings basement club.

Because if that win wouldn't come from within UEFA, well, San Marino would look without.

In March 2022 San Marino began a series of friendlies with nations from other confederations around the globe.

On March 28, 2022, they possibly over-reached a little by taking on Cape Verde, ranked 65 in the world, who had qualified for the African Cup of Nations in 2013, 2015, and 2021. Though losing two-nil to a side who would qualify for the 2023 AFCON, and then go on to reach the quarter finals could be seen as another moral victory, another mini-fable of sorts, it was still a defeat.

In September 2022 San Marino would play another African side in fellow FIFA-rankings 200-club member: the Seychelles.

An archipelago of some 115 islands, 800 miles east of the African mainland in the Indian Ocean, the Seychelles had last won a competitive international match in a two-nil African Cup of Nations qualifier against Lesotho in 2016.

Like San Marino, the Seychelles chose to look beyond their continental borders for a morale boosting victory and had found it with a one-nil friendly win over Sri Lanka in 2021.

For both San Marino and Seychelles, victory at the San Marino Stadium on September 22, 2022, would have been a major coup. As it turned out, neither side would prevail in a close nil-nil stalemate.

Two months later, and capitalising on the revitalised members in the lower reaches of CONCACAF – thanks to their own Nations League and the competitive fixtures it provided – San Marino would travel to Saint Lucia in the Caribbean for a double-header at the Daren Sammy Cricket Ground. And it was there on November 17, 2022, where Lorenzo Lazzari would score not only his first and only international goal to date, but the first San Marino goal ever scored outside Europe in a one-all draw in the first match.

Saint Lucia, who came bottom of their inaugural Nations League, League B group behind El Salvador, Montserrat, and Dominican Republic in 2019, but were then promoted straight back up into League B in 2022 by beating Anguilla and Dominica home and away in their League C campaign, finished a successful 2022 with a one-nil win over San Marino in the second friendly three days later. More than 3,000 cheered them on in a first-ever victory against a team outside of their confederation.

A draw and a narrow defeat were, yet again, more positives for San Marino against a side who would do more than hold their own in their 2023 CONCACAF Nations League, League B season, finishing second behind Guadeloupe, and above Sint Maarten and Saint Kitts and Nevis (who would lose four of their six matches as they were relegated to League C).

But a draw, a defeat wasn't what San Marino had been hoping for.

Perhaps against a side that Saint Lucia had beaten, San Marino would get their much-needed win…

In the early stages of preparation for the new 2024 Nations League season, and once again taking advantage of a CONCACAF team rejuvenated by regular, competitive Nations League football, San Marino hosted Saint Kitts and Nevis for a double header at the San Marino Stadium in March 2024.

Again, it would end in relative disappointment as Saint Kitts and Nevis ran out three-one winners in the first game. Tyquan Terrell, a home-based player with St Peters FC scored the equaliser after a Sammarinese penalty was converted by Filippo Berardi, before Andre Burley of National League Oxford City scored a second for the Sugar Boyz. Harry Panayioutou, who plays for Sirens in the Maltese Premier League finished off the win.

A nil-nil draw four days later proved yet again how competitive San Marino could be, but still no win.

But, possibly more importantly, the two sets of fixtures against Saint Lucia and Saint Kitts and Nevis proved that taking advantage of opportunities against their Caribbean Nations League cousins could be a new avenue of competition in the search for that illusive, transformational victory.

And, if not that, then at least they could collect more little fables for the republic, such as Berardi's first ever Sammarinese goal outside of Europe.

Two further friendly defeats to Slovakia and Cyprus in the summer of 2024 meant that San Marino would face down their 2024 Nations League season on a 140-game, 20-year winless streak.

Despite their best, wide-reaching and inventive efforts.

Maybe next time, it could be Anguilla calling? Or possibly a new initiative trialled by FIFA to aid those countries near the foot of their prospective confederations' rankings with opportunity, experience, and the chance to develop?

While San Marino took on Saint Kitts and Nevis in that double-header in March 2024 thanks to their own inventive and transformative outreach, another tournament of sorts was taking place – the FIFA World Series.

Designed to offer opportunity to nations from across the six football confederations of the world, the FIFA World Series pitted teams who would never normally play against one another – the idea being that these extra matches would enable development via exposure to different playing styles – they would also be a source of competitive football where many of the countries taking part had very limited opportunity to play at the international level.

This five-day football fiesta took place in host nations Algeria, Azerbaijan, Saudi Arabia (who hosted two groups) and Sri Lanka. Twenty nations in a world cup, the like of which had never been seen before in FIFA circles.

Andorra, Bolivia, and South Africa joined hosts Algeria in Algiers and Annaba. Bulgaria, Tanzania, and Mongolia travelled to Baku to play in a group hosted by Azerbaijan.

Cape Verde, Guyana, Equatorial Guinea, and Cambodia made up one of the groups in Jeddah, Saudi Arabia. Guinea, Brunei, Bermuda, and Vanuatu made up the second.

A final group based in Colombo, Sri Lanka, saw the Central African Republic, Papua New Guinea and Bhutan join the hosts.

The outcome of pitting these unlikely bedfellows together was a largely even and competitive set of results.

Only Guinea's six-nil victory over Oceanic Vanuatu and their five-one win against Caribbean Bermuda, coupled with the Central African Republic's six-nil win over Himalayan Bhutan stood out as heavy defeats.

Even so, the experience was far from negative for these sides, with Bermuda also picking up a two-nil win over Brunei, Vanuatu only losing three-two to Brunei courtesy of a 94th minute winner from Hakeme Yazid Said (who plays his club football for Duli Penigiran Muda Mahkota FC in the Singapore Premier League), and Bhutan losing narrowly to Sri Lanka at the Colombo Racecourse in front of more than 6,000 supporters.

Elsewhere Bolivia beat Andorra by a single goal, Tanzania beat Mongolia three-nil, while Equatorial Guinea beat Cambodia two-nil.

Meanwhile Sri Lanka drew with Papua New Guinea nil-nil and Cape Verde beat Guyana with a single goal in the second minute. Ryan Mendes, who played 35 games for Nottingham Forest in the 2015/16 season, but who now represents Kocaelispor in the Turkish second tier, scored the early winner.

In the most likely, and least inspiring of the fixtures, Azerbaijan held fellow Europeans Bulgaria one-all – both teams sharing top spot in their group after one-nil wins over Mongolia and Tanzania respectively.

Beyond that, the series had been a universal success, delivering what it had set out to do for many footballing nations deprived of regular, competitive international football. So much so that a second series in 2026 has been confirmed, with the possibility of it appearing every even year after that.

Nations such as San Marino and Anguilla must be sure bets for this next series. They would be perfect, and no doubt most-willing participants, given what such an opportunity could potentially do for both.

But should they be offered a place it would remain to be seen whether they would still go into it on winless streaks. Because for them both, a new Nations League season loomed on the horizon.

For Anguilla that meant fixtures against Belize and the Turks and Caicos Islands, and San Marino facing down Gibraltar.

But, before then, for the Sammarinese, their new Nations League adventure begins at home to the UEFA nation with the second longest winless streak, and the only team they have ever beaten – Liechtenstein…

If a football fan was asked to think about San Marino, chances are that, if anything sprang to mind at all other than "the worst team in the world," it would probably be one of two things – or rather, people.

Think of San Marino and you think of Davide Gualtieri's goal after just 8.3 seconds that humiliated England in November 1993. To make matters worse for England, or elevate the Sammarinese mini-fable even higher, it was the fastest ever international goal scored, and remained in the record books as such for 23 years (until Christian Benteke scored for Belgium against Gibraltar in 2016 after 8.1 seconds).

Despite a final scoreline of seven-one, the damage had been done – England failed to qualify for the 1994 World Cup after Holland beat Poland to put the qualifying spots beyond them, and Davide Gualtieri's goal became a symbol of that failure.

If that Gualtieri goal doesn't spring to mind when asked to think of the San Marino National Football Team, one by Andy Selva possibly does.

When Andy Selva retired from international football on 73 caps for his country in 2016, the news – like Elia Benedettini's eight years later – passed almost without acknowledgement beyond San Marino's tiny border. His name only remaining where others faded into world football obscurity due to his position as his countries all-time leading goal scorer.

However, his name, his record of eight goals in 73 appearances, while rightly celebrated within San Marino, has become a stick to beat the national team with by lazy journalists from some of Europe's biggest and best footballing nations – bemoaning fixtures against such minnows. Andy Selva, his record, would be resurrected time and again, with every match, to highlight the gulf in class. The fact that his eight goals accounted for just about one quarter of all San Marino's goals ever scored in international football, a joke.

Thankfully Sammarinese football, indeed football within all minnow nations don't see it like that. Selva's goal scoring record, like those of all leading goal scorers from nations in Group D of the Nations League, tell a story of courage, perseverance, and no small amount of ability to score against world class defenders and goalkeepers playing in top leagues around the continent.

Of Andy Selva's eight goals, seven were scored in competitive fixtures. His first came in October 1998 against Austria in a Euro 2000 qualifier. His second would come two and a half years later in a chastening 10-1 defeat away to Belgium in a World Cup qualifier. But better was to come in the return fixture in June 2001, where he would equalise to make it one-all before Belgium came back to win four-one.

It would be four years until his next competitive goal – another equaliser against Belgium in March 2005 in another World Cup qualifier. This time Belgium would struggle but would eventually come away with a two-one win. Three months later, Selva scored against Bosnia and Herzegovina in a three-one defeat.

His penultimate international goal came in a two-one defeat to Wales in October 2007, before his final goal in a three-one loss to Slovakia in October 2008.

That night to forget in 2001 at the King Baudouin Stadium, Brussels aside: six competitive fixtures against good national teams with some exceptional talent on display. To score against them speaks of a tenacity, passion, and a skill often overlooked – not only in Selva, but in his team-mates who got him into those scoring positions.

Totals that may seem humble to some. But put into the correct perspective – a genuine perspective – Andy Selva's exploits deserve to be remembered as the incredible achievements they are.

But of all his eight goals, it is, no doubt, the one he scored in a friendly fixture that stands out above all the others. For its significance stretches far beyond the standard Sammarinese mini fable, becoming legend.

On 28 April 2004, Selva would score the only goal of the game in a friendly win over Liechtenstein. The first ever win in international football for San Marino, ending a wait of 18 years since that first ever match against Canada Under-23's back in 1986.

Record goal scorer for his country, solid striker in Italy's Serie C with Bellaria, SPAL 1907, and Sassuolo, Selva could be remembered first and foremost for either, were it not for that night in 2004.

He has been in a select group of one ever since.

For 20 long years.

The only person to ever score a winner for the San Marino Men's National Team.

Before the 2024 Nations League got under way, there had been 140 matches since Andy Selva's heroics in 2004. Among them some near misses, some moments when San Marino got so close to another win.

In 2014 they picked up only their third ever point in a qualifying campaign with a goalless draw at home to Estonia. In the Nations League in 2020 they picked up goalless draws against Gibraltar and Liechtenstein. Points number four and five.

Elsewhere in those 140 games there have been some narrow defeats, and some not so narrow defeats. But slowly, thanks to the Nations League, and a campaign of friendly matches, in recent years deficits have reduced even further – with fine margins defining results – and with them a sense of momentum, belief has begun to grow.

With hope, a little expectation has been added, especially after the draw for the 2024 Nations League pitted the Sammarinese up against Gibraltar, and Liechtenstein – the European nations closest to them in the FIFA World Rankings. Closest to them in population size, land mass, and footballing history.

Within Sammarinese footballing circles, and thanks to such progression on the field, the Nations League draw, a question has bubbled to the surface:

If not now, when?

When will there be a better time to break that 140-game winless run. And have someone else join Andy Selva in that select club of Sammarinese match-winners? And even go one further, becoming the first ever Sammarinese to score the winning goal in a competitive fixture. Claiming three points.

Going top of the table.

After all that hard work. All that sacrifice, dedication, endeavour, progression.

If not now, when?

The capital of San Marino, also called San Marino – population 4,000 (the fifth smallest capital population in the world), a UNESCO World Heritage Site dating back to 301 CE – is beguiling in the late summer sun.

Narrow labyrinthine alleyways tumble away across the steep sides of Monte Titano in lung burning switchbacks; most far too narrow for vehicles, visitors lean into the cobbles, the paving slabs to ascend them, pausing to look up at the beautiful old-shuttered buildings seemingly stacked on top of each other. Neighbours from the street above looming down, looking out on a sea of terracotta roofs tiles. Myriad tiled balconies, bell towers, chimneys, porches, walls, lean-tos scatter in a patchwork of weathered reds, browns, greys and greens across the peaked roofs of San Marino. A chaotic geometrical marvel, it is as breathtaking as the inclines that slice through them.

It is picturesque, unique, and befitting its heritage status. It is also magical, confounding, disorienting.

Every alleyway seems so very similar to the one you just left. Sometimes only subtle differences mark them out, making it very easy to become lost. Retracing your steps taking you into a little street that now has a café on the corner. The door to your hotel somehow vanished. The tourist map seemingly not including every side street and alley, letting you stumble into some uncharted territory. Turning you around. Sending you in what seems the right direction, but not quite.

San Marino is a living, working, bustling maze, where nowhere is found the first time, but is discovered, eventually. And your return never appears to follow that path you took to get there. But get there you do, eventually.

Ascending the labyrinth up to the peaked spine of San Marino, and the three towers of Guaita, Cesta, and Montale – the first of which has been guarding this serene republic for the best part of a millenium – you finally see the bigger picture of the capital laid out beneath you. No less confusing. But at least with all its intricacies, contradictions, and idiosyncrasies before you.

From the battlements linking the towers together, teetering on top of a sheer rocky drop, littered with trees and shrub that have somehow gained purchase, defying gravity and logic, Monte Titano plummets down to the town of Borgo Maggiore below.

The last (or first, depending on which way you are going) of the grand peaks of the Apennine Mountains, from its top Rimini and the Adriatic Sea shimmer in the distance.

From such a vantage point you can trace the journey Saint Marinus took some 1,700 years earlier in his quest for religious sanctuary.

From such a position you can also watch the progress of pilgrims of another kind, following in his footsteps, making their way from Rimini Airport to this most magical of capitals.

Buses pause to let their passengers off, among them, football fans wearing shirts from Scotland (and more impressively the Highlands of Scotland via Ross County and Inverness Caledonian Thistle), Finland, Holland, England, Italy and Germany – all step out into the hot sun on the ultimate European footballing minnow's pilgrimage.

They come in hope – like the Sammarinese, when it comes to their team, there is always hope. For a good performance, a mini fable, maybe even a goal.

But, like the Sammarinese gathered in cafes, like the shop keepers selling San Marino flags, shirts, scarves – this time, mingling with that hope, a new element has manifested.

Possibly for the first time ever, a feeling of expectation is growing over espressos and cigarette smoke. That maybe, just maybe, San Marino could win a football match. A first-ever competitive football match. In just a few hours' time.

Joining the Sammarinese, football romantics from around the continent have come, a steady trickle arriving, losing themselves in the tangle of streets beyond the bus stop, in the hope of seeing something special. Something no-one has ever seen before…

The Nations League draw had been as kind as it could have been. The six teams that would make up the two groups in League D were split with each cluster as close to one another in the FIFA world rankings as they could possibly be.

In Group D2 Malta, ranked 172 in the world, were joined by Andorra (164) and Moldova (152), leaving group D1 with an intriguing trio of San Marino (210th and last), Liechtenstein (199) and Gibraltar (198).

Gibraltar only joined UEFA in 2013 and FIFA in 2016. Their applications to become members before those dates rejected, in no small part due to Spain's objections, who lay claim to the 2.6 square mile tip of the Iberian Peninsula (that juts out into the strait of Gibraltar – the mouth to the Mediterranean – a mere 7.7 nautical miles from the continent of Africa).

Before these political obstacles were overcome, the national team plied their footballing trade in non-FIFA competitions such as the Island Games against the likes of the Shetland Isles, Greenland, the Isle of Wight, and Guernsey.

In 2013 they began life in UEFA with a goalless draw in a friendly match against Slovakia, held in Portugal while their national stadium was brought up to standard for international football.

A first win followed in 2014 with a one-nil friendly win over Malta, but it wouldn't be until 2018 that Gibraltar enjoyed victory on home soil, beating Latvia one-nil at the newly revamped Victoria Stadium.

Up to and including qualification for Euro 2024, Gibraltar have never won a competitive fixture in any of the World Cup or European Championship campaigns they have taken part in.

In Euro 2024 qualifying they experienced the full spectrum of emotion with respectable three-nil defeats to France, Holland, Greece, and the Republic of Ireland. They also suffered their heaviest ever defeat, losing 14-0 to France in front of 32,000 in Nice.

In the Nations League, however, Gibraltar have fared much better.

In 2018 they secured their first and second ever competitive wins in the space of four days, beating Armenia one nil in Yerevan on October 13, before securing a first competitive victory on home soil with a two-nil win over Liechtenstein on October 16.

Better would come in the 2020 edition with a two nil home victory over San Marino in September, followed up with a one nil win away to Liechtenstein in October. Two draws in the return matches saw Gibraltar top the group, winning promotion to League C for the 2022 competition.

In a tough group containing Bulgaria, Georgia, and North Macedonia they picked up a solitary point with a one all draw at home to Bulgaria. But a two-nil defeat at home to North Macedonia, and a two one loss at the Victoria Stadium to a Georgian side who would go on to top the group showed that Gibraltar could at least mix it with some bigger footballing nations.

Indeed, their close-fought game with Georgia took on extra significance when Georgia qualified for Euro 2024 via a play-off between the four Nations League Group C winners (beating Luxembourg in the semi-final before overcoming Greece on penalties in the final). Then again when Georgia drew with Czechia and beat Portugal to qualify for the knock-out stages, before putting up a spirited performance against eventual winners Spain in the round of 16.

Aside from that terrible night in Nice, Gibraltar could look forward to the 2024 Nations League with a confidence and expectation that their performances and results warranted.

One place below Gibraltar in the FIFA world rankings, 199th out of 210, stands Liechtenstein.

Another of Europe's micro-states at just 62 square miles, sandwiched among the high peaks of the Alps between Austria to the east and north, and Switzerland to the west and south, Liechtenstein's population of 40,000 is 6,000 stronger than both Gibraltar and San Marino.

Of the three, they were the first to enter the international football fray in June 1981 in the unlikely setting of the Presidents Cup in South Korea.

Ludwig Sklarski became the first ever Liechtensteiner to score for his country in a one-all draw against Malta in their opening game. And after a two-nil defeat to Thailand, Donat Marxer would score a hat trick against Indonesia to become not only the first player from Liechtenstein to ever achieve the feat – only Martin Stoklasa has done so since, in a three-all friendly draw with Luxembourg in 2002. Marxer was also the first Liechtensteiner to ever score the winner for his homeland; something that has only ever happened 14 other times in the 43 years since, and only eight times in competitive fixtures.

It would take until October 1998 for Liechtenstein to notch up three points in a qualifying campaign, Martin Telser scoring the winner in a two-one win over Azerbaijan in a Euro 2000 qualifier.

In 2004 and 2005, Liechtenstein would do the double over Luxembourg in their World Cup qualifying group, and 2007 would go down as the nation's most prolific year, beating both Iceland and Latvia in the qualifying campaign for Euro 2008.

It would take another seven years for the next win, one-nil over Moldova in 2014, and another four after that to see Liechtenstein taste victory again in a two nil Nations League win over Gibraltar in 2018.

In 2020 Liechtenstein would beat San Marino two-nil in their Nations League group, and after a two-one friendly win in October 2020 over Luxembourg, Liechtenstein would embark on a 40-game winless run.

Losing nine of their ten World Cup 2022 qualifiers – a one-all draw against Armenia in Yerevan their only point, with Noah Frick's 80th minute equaliser, the second and last Liechtenstein goal scored all campaign (his elder brother Yanick Frick scored in a four-one home loss against Iceland) – Liechtenstein would fare no better in their 2022 Nations League group.

Six defeats, albeit very narrow defeats, against group winners Latvia (one-nil and two-nil), Moldova (two-nil home and away) and Andorra (two-one in Andorra La Vella with Livio Meier scoring Liechtenstein's only goal of the campaign, and a two-nil loss at home), saw Liechtenstein competitive, but winless.

Euro 2024 qualifying saw Liechtenstein remain largely competitive (four-nil defeats away at both Portugal and Iceland, and a seven-nil drubbing at home to Iceland excepting), but still winless. A sole Sandro Wolfinger goal in a two-one loss to Bosnia and Herzegovina in Zenica, the sum total in Liechtenstein's plus column in another pointless campaign.

And while 2024 started off in a rocky fashion with a four-nil friendly defeat in Marbella to the Faroe Islands, better was to come four days later with a one-all friendly draw in Cyprus against Latvia.

And two close-fought friendlies against Euros-bound Albania and Romania in June 2024 gave the Liechtensteiners something to build on in preparation for this new Nations League season.

After all, the draw had been kind to them too. Competitive matches from the 2022 campaign, and solid performances since, giving them something to believe in.

Especially when Liechtenstein's four-year record of 40 international matches of any kind without a win is dwarfed by their hosts 20-year, 140 match winless streak.

As always, hope springs eternal. But with that hope, for Liechtenstein as well as San Marino, a sense of opportunity is in the air. A chance to create something special. Something others take for granted.

But not here. Not among the mystifying weave of ancient Sammarinese streets.

Hope. But now, also, genuine opportunity.

Opportunity only heightened by heroics performed far away, from a fellow member of the FIFA world rankings basement club.

On the eve of the San Marino – Liechtenstein match, thousands of miles across the Atlantic Ocean on Providenciales in the Turks and Caicos islands, Anguilla finally banished their own footballing demons in their opening 2024 CONCACAF Nations League fixture.

After 48 competitive fixtures without a win, stretching back to 2010, Anguilla, ranked 209 out of 210 in the world, tasted victory.

National team captain Germain Hughes – alumnus of Anguillan club side Roaring Lions, but now elevated to the Trinidad and Tobago Premier

League with Cunupia – led from the front by scoring his second-ever international goal in the 57th minute to put his nation on the brink.

A second from Lamar Carpenter sealed the win, and a first ever three-point haul in the Nations League.

And, just like that, the world's second worst winless run was over – isolating San Marino that little bit further, and relegating Liechtenstein down to the second worst record in world football.

The social media congratulations to Anguilla from other minnow nations around the world felt genuine. A win, for one, feeling like a win for all, boosting that hope, that sense of what can be achieved, if hard work, humility, and perseverance can be maintained.

As the light faded, the grand towers of Guaita, Cesta, Montale loomed in the growing darkness over the maze of terracotta roofs of San Marino.

They stood over the town, the nation, as they have stood for what feels like all time – their rough-hewn stone walls seemingly as ageless as the Apennines surrounding them. Their peaks visible from virtually every point within the republic.

They stood, and as the town settled down beneath them, they loomed in the darkness, and waited, for whatever tomorrow might bring…

For possibly the first time ever, a San Marino national team press conference attempts to play down expectations. Not dampen the mood, but lay down the foundations for the battle to come – a battle so finely matched it is hard to call – in case the result does not go their way.

Roberto Cevoli, national team manager does his best:

The topic of injuries is becoming a recurring one. And here they have a greater impact than in other footballing realities, because we do not have such a large pool of players.

Nonetheless, I am more than happy and confident in the players who are with us, especially the younger ones who are eager and raring to show their worth – this gives me pride.

Expectations are still high. Since the (Nations League Group) *draw in Paris we have been thinking about this match, and the work done so far has been in view of this match* (against Liechtenstein).

As always, it will be a difficult match, but still with a team that, in my opinion, could be within our reach.

Clearly, the pitch will tell whether this will actually be the case.

Cevoli isn't playing his "injuries and young players card" without reason. National team retirements and injuries to established internationals have forced the promotion of no less than five players into the starting eleven with four senior caps or less.

Goalkeeper Edoardo Colombo has four international appearances to his name. His understudy, Matteo Zavoli has none. In front of him in defence will be 18-year-old Giacomo Benvenuti, making his national team debut.

In midfield, Andrea Contadini will be the senior partner to Matteo Valli Casadei, his four caps outshining Casedei's solitary appearance for the Titans. And helping to lead the line will be 19-year-old Nicko Sensoli, with three San Marino caps to his name.

This changing of the guard has stripped San Marino of some battle-hardened players and has left the squad with just four international goals between the 23. But what it has also done is open the door to a set of players with, maybe for the first time in Sammarinese history, a completely different mindset.

These players, fresh out of the youth ranks, have come up through the system watching San Marino play close-fought and competitive fixtures across three Nations League campaigns since 2018.

They saw Nicola Nanni's heartbreak at that overturned penalty against Malta in 2022 – the difference between the sides that day. They saw that desperately close miss, right at the death, in Ta-Qali a week later. For them, maybe the prospect of winning for San Marino is not quite so abstract, or psychologically challenging as their forebears. The hard work laid down ahead of them helping to change the mindset a little.

Enabling with that hope, a little expectation borne out of regular, consistently close-fought games. Games where only the width of a post, or a marginal VAR decision denied them that chance of glory.

In the press conference, captain Alessandro Golinucci (and elder statesman of the squad after 94-cap Matteo Vitaioli became the latest to pull-out through a muscle tear) tried to use the experience gained from his 51 international appearances to balance this youthful exuberance with pragmatism:

> *It is one of those games where both teams can think about winning and will do everything to succeed. We're playing at home, and we have to make our stadium an extra weapon.*
>
> *Our goal is to put a lot of competitive spirit on the pitch and exploit the talents of many of our young players, who are capable of hurting Liechtenstein.*

> *The first commandment – in this sense – is to avoid defensive errors. The most recent games against them were decided by the smallest margin, so the game is more about incidents.*
>
> *First of all, we want to show that we are compact, because then up front we have players who are capable of creating danger for their defence.*

Somewhere between these two philosophies of defensive rigour and youthful attacking flair, Golinucci, Cevoli, and the rest of the Sammarinese team hope that success that way lies. And as the sun rises on match-day, amid clock watching and the interminable slow procession of the hours before kick-off, players and supporters alike attempt to traverse this calm before that evening's footballing storm.

The hours are filled, as it turned out, with an actual storm. An ungodly thunderstorm watched on by throngs of tourists on viewing platforms and from the battlements atop Guiata and Cesta. A dark, impenetrable veil of bleak swirling rain, swallowing up the mountains of the Apennines, the sky turning from day to night. Birds in the trees silenced as this dusk fell. The hush amplifying the violence when it came.

As the storm rolled in, its enormity devouring everything before it, a nervousness, a shifting among the watchers.

When it finally came, the rain came down in sheets so thick it dissolved the view, drumming on rooftops, pounding the cobbled streets, sending everyone scattering, flinching, as deafening thunderclaps clapped and boomed and brilliant forked lightning lit up the scene, then sent it back into darkness.

The violence humbling, everyone cowered as best they could from the worst of it, for what seemed like ages – the lightning fizzing and crackling, the thunder so profound it seemed like the very foundations of San Marino were shaking – until, finally, the pounding rain began to ease, the darkness fade, and the storm passed, sweeping on and away toward Rimini, the Adriatic coast.

The sun came back out. As did the tourists, the locals. And started about their days again, as if nothing had happened. The rivulets of rainwater gurgling and surging through the steep maze of alleyways, down toward the foot of Monte Titano, the only reminder that it had ever been here.

As the hours toward kick-off wound down, the heat began to rise again. Not with the intensity of high summer, this early September evening, but with enough warmth to keep everyone gathering outside the San Marino stadium in Serravalle in t-shirts and shorts.

One last hurrah before the changing of the seasons – as it turned out, both meteorological and sporting in Serravalle.

A quirk of San Marino city's perilous position across the sheer sides of Monte Titano is that expansion is nigh on impossible. The streets of five centuries ago are the streets of today. Geography dictates this. And there is no scope for football pitches.

So, as San Marino's population and sporting aspirations grew, it was elsewhere they made home, such as Serravalle.

Nestled among the flat lands of northern San Marino, Serravalle's population of 10,000 dwarfs the nation's capital two and half times over.

As with everywhere in San Marino, Monte Titano and it's three towers loom in the distance, foreshortening the ten kilometres of winding road between them, creating a fittingly dramatic backdrop to the nations sporting endeavours – most of which can be found in one location in Serravalle at an immaculate sports park.

Containing the national football stadium, complete with an athletics track, and a building featuring an Olympic size swimming pool and courts of various sporting hues, it is the far end of the park that epitomises this passing of the sporting guard from summer to autumn, and beyond.

In the San Marino baseball park, empty bleachers stand dormant, batting nets hang limp.

A peeling poster of the summer's now complete fixtures on the side of the shuttered fan shop flutters on the slight breeze.

A few players in practice gear wander out into back field by the scoreboard, throwing a ball between them with a lack-lustre born out of no competitive edge. As ball thuds into weathered leather mitts there is no heat, no speed. It is routine without that prospect of sporting battle. One last stretch of the arm before everything is mothballed for the winter, and those floodlights cut out. Players, distracted, looking across at the floodlights of the national stadium, the sounds of music playing. The passing of the baton…

It is a hive of activity around the national stadium. A walking football game between supporters of San Marino and Liechtenstein plays out in the car park. Next door young children are scuffing and rushing between two small goals, arms raised if they find them, laughs if they don't, chasing after the ball to retrieve it. A small group of San Marino's national team youth section are juggling a ball between them, their flicks and tricks making people pause to watch, as is a small marquee with a couple of monitors linked up to a football computer game, the muted roars of a simulated crowd.

If there is any anxiety about the impending match, it is not on display here.

The walking football match complete, opposing players decked out in a spread of national team shirt vintages, both home and away, mingle and take selfies with one another. Walk together round to the gates in readiness for the game, wave as the Liechtenstein supporters head up to their spot in the far-left hand side of the main stand, while the Sammarinese supporting Brigata Mai Uno Gioia head to their usual spot at the far-right end.

There is no need for segregation, and there is none. The stand is open, people come and go, taking photographs with opposing supporters. Shirts, flags draped across empty seats, chants, they are simply a display of pride and passion and are received as such with a respect and magnanimity by those Sammarinese sat around their Liechtensteiner neighbours.

No matter the importance of the match, the meaning it has for players and supporters alike – that opportunity to arrest a win-less run, to start a new era in their national team's history – it will be played out, off and on the pitch, with a deference and courtesy that speaks of two nations who are already winning, in so many ways.

Just not always out on the pitch.

While the Liechtenstein fans settle in, applauding their heroes out onto the pitch as they begin their warm-up, so too do the Brigata Mai Uno Gioia, using gaffer tape to put up their own banners on the back wall of their block (that is littered with the remnants of past gaffer tape fixings that have pulled at the paintwork, left adhesive marks – these scars a tapestry of years of dedication, often without much joy, in supporting their national team).

As a supporter group, the Brigata Mai Uno Gioia – just like their Liechtensteiner counterparts across the stand – are as benign a group as you could hope to meet.

Two men of an age that predates San Marino's entry into FIFA by at least a decade stand beaming. Looking out across the pristine pitch, the evening sky ablaze – lit up orange, red and indigo as the last light from the setting sun, long since dropped beneath the brow of the Apennines, it creates a spectacular backdrop worthy of a few moments' contemplation, appreciation.

The hills between the beautiful night sky and the brilliant emerald green of the floodlit pitch stand blackened as night descends, partitioning one spectacular sight from the other – the two men, wearing vintage San

Marino national team shirts look out, while the Brigata Mai Uno Gioia begin to congregate around them.

'We don't care where you are from. If you are here for San Marino, then you are welcome to stand with us', one said with a welcoming smile. 'You don't even need to sing and clap. Just being here, among this group gives the players encouragement. Knowing that you are here for them. We encourage as many as we can to come with us.'

And come with them they do, in ones and twos. A smattering of Sammarinese regulars (including one with an English accent who had clearly become enamoured with San Marino a long time ago, judging by his old, journeyed San Marino shirt) joined by many of those football fans who had wandered the ancient boundaries of the capital earlier in the day.

A group of German supporters, a group of English, Finnish, a man in a Dutch national team shirt, the Ross County and Inverness Caledonian Thistle supporters are also in close attendance – they come, by invitation of the Brigata, and stand in support of the tiny republic of San Marino.

It is all smiles, waves, laughter, so much so that the security guard at the back of stand seems more than redundant. Another point of pride for the Brigata and the Sammarinese.

When it is time for the players to walk out, the two men at the heart of San Marino's supporter group take up their positions: one at the back by their banner, the other near the front – a small toy drum hanging from a strap around his neck perched on top his midriff – and with drumstick in one hand and a fragile-looking small plastic loud speaker in the other, he holds it up to his mouth and the Brigata Mai Uno Gioia welcome their heroes out onto the pitch to the tiny beat of the drum, and with a burst of well-used chants.

Across the stand, supporters rise to welcome the teams, the central blocks packed with children from San Marino's youth section and local teams, Elisa Terenzi and her Women's Under 16 side, along with members of San Marino Academy, boosting the attendance to close to 1,000.

Even so, there is no need for the stand on the far side of the pitch, which remains unopened and is draped in huge national flags and the football association's logo.

But, in a population of 35,000, 1,000 is impressive.

National anthems impeccably observed, albeit with a little consternation by some in attendance at Liechtenstein's 'Oben am jungen Rhein', which is set to the same melody as Britain's 'God Save the King'. Written in 1745, it had also been used by German-speaking nations such as Bavaria, Prussia and saxony as national anthems. Indeed, Switzerland only dispensed with it as the melody to their national anthem in 1961. But while

Switzerland dispensed, Liechtenstein persevered, causing the shrugging of shoulders among those not in the know as it played out into the late summer night.

Formalities over, the announcer helped the Brigata in whipping up the support in the stand as he read out the starting elevens.

With the Sammarinese eleven he would call out each player's first name, then encourage the supporters to join him in chanting their surnames – accentuating each syllable:

'Andrea CON-TA-DI-NI. Allesandro GOL-IN-U-CCI. Nicko SEN-SO-LI. Giacomo BEN-VEN-U-TI'.

Then, at the end, the announcer screamed 'FORZA TITANI', signalling the Brigata's conductor to beat out another chant on his little drum, led from the front through his toy loud-speaker.

Those few who knew the words sang along, those who didn't clapped along: this patchwork of support from across the continent.

The small numbers (even swelled by foreign imports the Brigata stood less than 100 strong), the smiles, the ages, the toy drum and speaker – they were a good-natured, welcoming, respectful, benign sight, cheering on their team.

But do not let benign somehow translate as lesser or insignificant. Do not let it fool you into thinking the Brigata Mai Uno Gioia aren't as passionate or dedicated as any other fan group from any other nation around the world.

Aggression isn't passion, just as being benign isn't a symptom of a lack of passion. Different nations do things in different ways. And one could argue with a degree of certainty that any fan group who travels home and away across Europe, despite not seeing a win of any kind for 20 years, must be the most passionate, most dedicated set of supporters in world football.

They just do things their way

And their way enables a young family to sit among them, a toddler decked out in a little San Marino shirt, skittering chaotically up and back along an empty row of seats, pausing every now and then – mesmerised – looking up at the singing and chanting, the beating of the drum. The hint of a smile surfacing among the wonder writ large across her face at the singing, synchronised clapping, the drum.

Her sister, maybe nine or ten, the San Marino blue and white daubed across each cheek, spends an equal amount of time making sure her sister doesn't stray too close to any steps, watching what is happening out on the pitch, and smiling up at the song and dance behind her.

It seems right, the balance struck. Benefitting all. Support in unison. For the players out on the pitch who, at the referee's whistle, set about to try and make history for their country.

It is the support they always receive from this small band, which they repay with endeavour and spirit.

But – and a consequence of the expectation this fixture has amassed – San Marino struggle to settle.

Liechtenstein set the tempo, passing the ball around with assurance, probing and testing the Sammarinese back line, who hold their own. But breaking down the Liechtenstein play, wrestling the ball back with precision tackles and towering headers, passing it out into midfield, results only in a couple of touches before San Marino lose it once more. It feels like they are just out of the groove, the inexperienced Sammarinese midfield, maybe distracted by the occasion. For 15, 20 minutes the game passes them by.

But while one element of San Marino's tactics stall – forwards Nicola Nanni and Nicko Sensoli as much spectators as the multi-national Brigata – another element stands firm: the defensive cohesion demanded by captain Alessandro Golinucci played out just as he had wanted.

The back four tackle, jostle, head and position themselves perfectly, repelling any Liechtenstein attack. And when winger Marcel Büchel got beyond them, whipping in a beautiful cross for Fabio Luque Notaro to sweep home past Edoardo Colombo in the Sammarinese goal, VAR proves that the San Marino line had held once more.

Bűchel had been offside. No goal.

And with that, something changed. And San Marino began to click.

Passes into midfield began to stick. Runs down the wing were found. Crosses into the forwards causing Liechtenstein problems.

A ball found Nicola Nanni, who jinked, set himself, and smashed the ball against the base of Benjamin Bűchel's post in the Liechtenstein goal. But before the rebound could be recycled, turned back into the danger area, the whistle went. The linesman's flag raised.

Liechtenstein too were holding their line well.

The first half played out on this knife-edge until the referee called time. A good 45 minutes for both teams. But the second would only be about one...

San Marino started the second half the way they had wanted to start the first, the midfield getting the ball, pushing the visitors back. Nanni and Sensoli up front darting into space looking for that killer pass that would send them through on goal. San Marino on top, holding the ball slightly better than Liechtenstein, they looked for that perfect pass.

But when opportunity came, it was all about instinct and desire, that subconscious drive forward – a symbiosis between hope and reality, making what could be a pointless run into a danger area, but doing it anyway, just in case – that separates the good from the average.

A ball is lofted toward the edge of the Liechtenstein box. There appears to be no danger. There are Liechtensteiner defenders, no Sammarinese strikers.

But Nicko Sensoli makes a run anyway.

The first Liechtenstein defender leaps to meet the ball. It is just a little too high, and his meeting with it only serves to flick the ball behind him. It loops into the box, where a second defender watches it begin to drop into the space between him and goalkeeper Benjamin Büchel. Both move toward it, neither sure who should lay claim to it. Both only seeing the flash of white shirt when it is too late.

Nicko Sensoli is there. He shouldn't have been. The situation could have made him stop running in, long before the ball had been flicked backwards by the defender.

But he didn't stop. He didn't stop when defender and goalkeeper converged on the ball. He knew, somehow, to keep going.

And as both Liechtensteiners hesitated, he did not, chipping the ball beautifully over Büchel's head toward goal.

Nineteen years old, only three national team appearances to his name – all of them friendlies – not even born when Andy Selva scored that winner against Liechtenstein back in 2004 – Sensoli didn't stop and watch the flight of the ball. He charged after it, as if willing it, chasing it into the net. Instinct again making him want to be first to any potential rebound.

Though no rebound came: his chipped lob nestling into the back of the net at the first time of asking.

Silence.

For a heartbeat.

Then pandemonium.

Sensoli, eyes wide, ran with his arms outstretched as far as he could until he was mobbed by his team-mates, both on the pitch, and by the wave of bodies rushing from the substitutes bench. Submerged beneath a heap of arms and legs.

In the stands disbelief at what they had seen quickly translated into guttural, primeval roars of that ever so rare commodity among the Brigata – joy.

The Brigata's conductor stood, arms raised, toy loud-speaker in one hand, drumstick in the other, and tried to absorb every single tiny element of what was happening in front of him with watery eyes. While next to him, two other long-suffering members hugged each other as they jumped up and down.

The mother, father and nine-year-old daughter at the front leapt and cheered and waved at friends behind them, to the side of them, sharing the moment as far, and with as many as they could – while the youngest of the group looked up at the Brigata behind her in wonder, watching the explosion of emotion with that hint of a smile, that look of fascination.

She would probably not remember that moment, being so very young. But it would, that experience, no doubt, instil a deep-rooted, subconscious sense of something in her. Something gloriously Sammarinese. An unspoken, ingrained pride in who she was, and where she was from.

And remember the moment or not, she would always be able to say that she was there. There the night Sensoli scored.

The rest, as they say, is history.

The last half hour of the match, and then another seven minutes added time could have been torturous. But it wasn't.

For most of it, San Marino remained in control. And as Liechtenstein tried desperately to push for an equalizer, more space was created behind them, enabling San Marino to break away, threaten a second.

A shot pulled wide of the post, a cross not quite meeting its wide-open target, a defence-splitting pass cut out by a desperate, last-ditch sliding lunge – these were the fine margins preventing a more comprehensive scoreline.

And even though their team looked comfortable, the Brigata whistled their anguish at what was, for them, an eternity of added time. A footballing lifetime of seeing results slip away at the last moment, by the tiniest of fractions, turning into near misses, haunting them, even now. As they stood, right on the cusp.

Their whistling anguished, but also impatient. Wanting history to be made. All the endeavour rewarded. For that 140-game win-less run to be over. For that first ever competitive victory. For Andy Selva to be joined in his select club of Sammarinese match-winners.

To be usurped, overshadowed a little by a new select club – of Sammarinese *competitive* match winners.

Just one whistle from the referee and it would all be theirs.

And then, finally, that whistle came.

Some of the more senior players simply sank to their knees. Floored by the enormity of what had been achieved, finally, after a career of trying. Others ran to colleagues, hugging one another. Others just ran. Lost in the emotion of it all, before being caught by substitutes, support staff who had poured onto the pitch.

Hugging, laughing, crying. Waving to family and friends in the stand that had been overrun by children, who pressed themselves against the Perspex barrier at the front, getting as close to their heroes as they could. As close to history before them, while the players tried to find their loved ones among the chaos playing out across the rows of seats, to share the moment, even if only with a look, a glance – something to connect them in this special moment, if only for an instant.

Then, in an almost unspoken, instinctive hive mind, the players made for the block housing the Brigata Mai Uno Gioia. They formed a line, holding hands, ran toward them, leaping in the air as they reached the touchline – fists pumping the air, hands clasped together in supplication at the feet of those who had supported them, no matter what. All those years.

The players knew this moment was as much theirs as it was anyone's. That without them it maybe would never have happened – this small, but unwavering support that extra percent. That tiny extra factor, like Nicko Sensoli's perseverance when others faltered. A perseverance that now had him floored, frozen as a chant raised up among the children:

'SEN-SOLI – SEN-SOLI – SEN-SOLI'.

Not in his wildest dreams…

The Brigata's conductor, his lieutenants, fellow Sammarinese supporters about them, and the Sammarinese for a day clapped and roared and cried and laughed and didn't know what to do.

Just as the players didn't.

They stood, facing one another, shaking heads, still in disbelief. Hugging whoever was closest, rubbing at teary eyes.

Neither group wanted to yield, to leave their spot, to have this moment finished. So, they stayed, looked at one another in wonder and awe.

It seemed right to leave them to it. Let those who had struggled together, for 20 years, to have this moment together, for as long as they needed it.

Slipping away, with one final glance back, beyond the celebrations, the Liechtenstein players stood forlornly in the centre circle. Heads bowed, shoulders drooped, broken, they stood. This had been more than simply a defeat. This loss saw them become the nation with the longest win-less run. Forty games and counting.

And as the story of San Marino's win travelled across news cycles around the world, they would be the fall guys. The joke.

They did not deserve that. As San Marino hadn't before them.

They had fought bravely, and as Alessandro Golinucci had predicted in his press conference, it had been a game of moments. And the decisive one had not gone their way.

At least there would be no time to dwell. They had a plane to catch. To Gibraltar. And another Nations League fixture in just three days' time.

(It would be a story of redemption, if not completely, then at least partially. A moral victory given the drama of added time.

Ferhat Saglam's 53rd minute equaliser had looked to have earned Liechtenstein a point. But then, on 97 minutes, Manchester United youth team player James Scanlon put Gibraltar ahead. Then in the 14th minute of added time, penalty to Liechtenstein. Captain Nicolas Hasler took the responsibility, slotted it home, and the international window without any joy for Liechtenstein suddenly had some.

And despite defeat to San Marino, the group was still wide open, with two home games remaining. Destiny, it was still the preserve of all three nations…)

Walking away from the San Marino stadium, leaning into the hill above it, the pitch shimmered an emerald green beneath the floodlights. The sounds of a tinny drumbeat, a loud-speaker, chants, clapping, drifted up into the night sky. Not quite ready to let go. Just a little longer, this new-found joy.

Back up among the battlements of the capital, the national stadium remained bathed in light – though the drumbeats, the singing had long since been dimmed by distance, though no doubt they were still out there, somewhere, celebrations drifting up into the night.

A jewel among the darkness – the stadium a beacon of national pride shining brightly up into the sky.

And for once, the whole world had taken notice.

Away, out past Rimini, over the Adriatic Sea, an electrical storm produced a spectacular light show. Lightning forks in reds and oranges lit up the darkness in a grand scale. Scything silently across the horizon beneath black, looming cloud.

A mute firework display worthy of the celebrations below.

Worthy of this confounding, unique, and timeless place. With its own football culture. Its own fables, heroes. And now, finally, its own success.

One hundred and forty no more.

Twenty years no more.

And despite their national team remaining 210th out of 210 in the FIFA World Rankings when the list is updated after the international break. Despite the rest of the footballing world finding themselves still standing on the shoulders of Titans, something fundamental has changed. Something seismic, if only within this tiny Republic.

Now, with hope, comes a belief.

Not that San Marino will suddenly become world beaters.

But a belief that they can be something more than simply competitive.

Especially in the Nations League.

Because San Marino.
Are *top* of the League.
Undefeated…

Line-ups: 5.09.24, San Marino Stadium,

San Marino

1 Eduardo Colombo
4 Giacomo Benvenuti
5 Michele Cevoli
6 Dante Rossi
9 Nicola Nanni (Nicolas Giacopetti 71')
10 Lorenzo Capicchioni (Marcello Mularoni 80')
11 Andrea Contadini
12 Alessandro Tosi (Tommaso Benvenuti 71')
17 Alessandro Golinucci © (Michael Battistini 62')
20 Nicko Sensoli (1) (Samuele Zannoni 62')
23 Matteo Valli Casadei

Liechtenstein

1 Benjamin Büchel
3 Max Göppel (Felix Oberwaditzer 62')
5 Niklas Beck (Martin Marxer 62')
7 Marcel Büchel
8 Aron Sele (Simon Lüchinger 62')
9 Ferhat Saglam
10 Sandro Wieser
16 Fabio Luque Notaro (Jonas Beck 81')
18 Nicolas Hasler ©
19 Emanuel Zünd (Livio Meier 62')
20 Sandro Wolfinger

Nations League D Group One

05.09.24 – San Marino 1 Liechtenstein 0
08.09.24 – Gibraltar 2 Liechtenstein 2

	P	W	D	L	F	A	Pts
San Marino	1	1	0	0	1	0	3
Gibraltar	1	0	1	0	2	2	1
Liechtenstein	2	0	1	1	2	3	1

Chapter Eight – Moldova v Andorra
October 10, 2024

THE GENTLE CHIME of the bell, the flickering on of the fasten seatbelt sign jogged me from my daydreaming out the aeroplane window.

Below me, looming out of the cloud, I had been lost in the grand, mystical Carpathian Mountains, in the equally mystical Transylvania.

A place synonymous in famous stories with dark folklore, vampire legend, with sheer gorges and terrifying passes among monstrous, jagged mountains. Somewhere, down there, Castle Dracula, and one of the most horrifying, captivating, enduring characters of the past 125 years.

To see it, albeit from a distance, after decades of wonder thanks to Bram Stoker's novel, the countless film adaptations, it sent a shiver down my spine. After all, a story of such atmosphere and menace, it needed an equally dark, brooding muse. A home befitting the chilling descriptions in the book. A place to anchor the fear, the marvel. And in the Romanian Carpathians, in Transylvania, Stoker had found a perfect companion for his story, and his classic, eternal character. Even from 30,000 feet it manifested a chill aura about those shadowy peaks and passes.

And nothing, it seemed, could exist beyond these grand literary mountains, loaded with menace and dark tales. For me, they had always been the end of the line. As far as even Bram Stoker dare go.

But today, they were nothing of the sort. Today they were simply the weigh-point for the beginning of our descent. A descent into an equally beguiling, mystifying, and unknown region, complete with an internationally unrecognised, breakaway republic within a republic. Where overshooting your landing could quickly find a pilot and his passengers perilously close to the border with a warzone, and a neighbour fighting for its life.

A route seldom taken by tourists to a place not expecting them, as the plane began to cut down through the cloud cover, I couldn't help but imagine Stoker's protagonist, Jonathan Harker as he journeyed ever deeper into the unknown.

I fastened my seatbelt, sat back, and waited for my own, personal unknown…

In preparing for the trip, it was as if Moldova didn't exist. Or, if it was being acknowledged as existing, it was being overlooked and ignored. And it seemed willfully so.

In the vast array of travel books stacked across shelves from floor to ceiling, there were a great many books on what seemed to be far more obscure, niche destinations than Moldova.

An old travel guide for Romania once had a section on its close neighbour, but in the more recent editions – the editions now available – Moldova had been cut out.

When asking if a travel book existed on Moldova, I got consternation, and maybe a hint of concern, a recoiling of some kind at the idea.

I was reminded of Jonathan Harker when, in Stoker's story, he reached a coach house deep in the high mountains of Transylvania. I was reminded of the horror on the owner's face, on his wife's face, both earnestly trying to convince him not to go when he explained he was waiting for transport to Castle Dracula.

Harker was not put off. And neither was I, even after I had what seemed to me to be my own tacit warning about travelling there.

After three attempts at three different Bureau de Changes to get some Moldovan Lei before the trip. Three furrows of three brows. Three shakes of the head.

'No, we don't do that.'

'Can it be ordered in?'

'No.'

A fourth and final attempt elicited the most withering condemnation of my travel plans, when a woman close to retirement shook her head, studying me closely.

'In all my 30 years working at this Bureau de Change, no-one has ever asked for Moldovan Lei before.'

I smiled, nodded. Gave up.

Moldova as a defined, sentient entity can be dated back to the 14th Century, though its people, descended from the ancient Dacians, settled in the region long before the coming of Christ.

They endured, outlasted the Roman and Byzantine Empires, along with invasions by the Goths, Huns, Avars, Bulgars, Magyars, Pechenegs, Cumans, Mongols, and Tatars.

The Principality of Moldova was founded in 1346 and outlasted the geo-political forces that impacted it over the following centuries, being manipulated and influenced by Hungarian, Polish and Ottoman powers, Moldova entered its most tumultuous phase with the dawning of the 19th Century.

In 1812, the Ottoman Empire handed the Principality to the Russian Empire, where it was renamed Bessarabia. A political act more than 200 years ago, it has had profound implications for Moldova ever since.

In 1856 Bessarabia decided to unite with neighbouring Wallachia, forming the basis of what is modern Romania, but in 1878 Russian control was restored, lasting until the fall of the Czars and the Russian Empire, after which Bessarabia declared independence once more in 1918.

This new-found independence would not last long. The Russian revolution, the rise of Soviet Russia soon saw the Red Army take back Bessarabia, renaming it the Moldavian Autonomous Republic within the Ukrainian Soviet Socialist Republic.

In 1940, as a result of the Molotov-Ribbentrop Act – a treaty of non-aggression between Nazi Germany and the Soviet Union – Bessarabia was formally declared Soviet, with Romania forced to withdraw any claim.

For the next 50 years, the Moldavian Soviet Socialist Republic existed beneath the cowl of Communism, suffering periodic famine as excessive food delivery quotas demanded by Moscow left the local population without.

When the Soviet Union collapsed, Moldova quickly declared independence, and on 27 August 1991, the spectre of Communism and Russian control was finally banished.

Thanks in no small part to the Soviet infrastructure left behind however, Moldova remains one of the poorest countries in Europe.

Moldova's borders do not quite reach the Black Sea, so tourism has not grown.

Chișinău, the nation's capital, was only a small provincial town before the Soviet Union built upon it to create a regional hub for the Socialist Republic. As a result, sprawling Brutalist Soviet tower blocks and municipal buildings dominate.

The old-town, cultural enclaves and centres, the UNESCO World Heritage Sites that other capital cities boast, is missing here, because Chișinău was never meant to be a capital. It never had that status or history before the middle of the 20th Century. Its landmarks sought out by tourists are few and far between, spread out, almost hidden by the great socialist experiment loaded on top of it.

And encircling everything, on the outskirts out the capital, crumbling industrial complexes. Large chimney stacks painted in red and white hoops – a staple across the former Soviet nations – do nothing to ease a gloomy, unappetising picture to those unprepared to look deeper.

These are not the only issues Moldova has in enticing the outside world in.

Because Russian aggression still looms large here. Attempting to destabilise, derail, and ultimately consume Moldova once more.

Even before official independence was declared from the collapsing Soviet Union in 1991, resistance to life beyond Russia's influence solidified in the east of the country, bordering Ukraine.

As early as 1990 – before the Soviet Union fell – the Pridnestrovian Moldavian Soviet Socialist Republic was established, hoping to remain within the Soviet Union even if the rest of Moldova chose independence, or even a re-unification with Romania.

In March 1992, a five-month conflict broke out between the fledgling independent Moldova and its breakaway region, more commonly known as Transnistria, until a ceasefire agreement between Moldova, Transnistria and Russia was brokered. This stopped the fighting, but didn't resolve the dispute, which remains today, with Transnistria recognised as Moldovan by the world's international community that doesn't align itself with Moscow.

Since 1992 Russia has had a military force inside Transnistria, a force that has increased in recent years. And with the invasion of Ukraine, Transnistria is seen as being under military occupation by Russia. Albeit willingly.

During the early stages of Putin's invasion of Ukraine, it was feared that Russia intended to punch through Ukraine's coastal regions to create a land bridge to Transnistria – absorbing it into the newly evolving geographical boundaries of the motherland.

But the offensive stalled, was repelled, before it reached Odessa – the last stop before the Moldovan/Transnistrian border.

During the ongoing invasion of Ukraine, and, indeed, during the decades preceding it, Transnistria has benefitted from funding from Moscow, along with a suspected booming trade selling arms on the black market, while Moldova has struggled on, as the continent's poorest relative.

Putin's desire to reclaim what he sees as territories lost from the old Russian Empire, has seen Transnistria used as a base to destabilise or unduly influence Moldovan governments and public opinion, through bribery and misinformation campaigns. Inflated prices for Moldova, and reduced ones for Transnistria, attempting to convince Moldovans that life under Russian influence is preferable, and more beneficial than a closer relationship with the European Union and NATO – a move undertaken by successive Moldovan governments since 2016, culminating in a referendum to join to EU only a few days after Moldova's Nations League match with Andorra.

Russia's attempts to influence Moldovan politics and public opinion has not been subtle. Multiple attempts to fund politicians aligned to Russia's cause, installing puppet, pro-Putin governments have failed.

However, the Moldovan peoples' response to Russia's invasion of Ukraine is possibly the greatest setback in Putin's attempts to bring them into the fold.

Despite being the poorest country in Europe (a statistic only changed after two years of war in Ukraine, that dropped them to the foot of the economic table), and having little resource to offer, Moldova, and the Moldovan people welcomed more than 700,000 Ukrainian refugees into their country in 2022 after the invasion began.

As the war raged toward them, Moldovans opened their doors to house their neighbours fleeing the bloodshed.

And while some 600, 000 moved on toward Poland, Germany and other European nations offering refuge, more than 107,000 stayed in Moldova. And of them, 75% remain as guests in the homes of ordinary Moldovans.

Walking around Chișinău, cars with Ukrainian numberplates are commonplace.

Like Odessa, Moldova stood firm. Even in the face of misinformation campaigns, funded protests, and other attempts to undermine the national narrative.

Time will tell what the future holds for Moldova, and whether EU membership (the referendum to join the EU, while not binding, was won by the yes vote by the narrowest of margins amidst flagrant attempts to sway the vote towards no. Financial incentives were widely offered to vote against EU membership), maybe even NATO membership enables them to finally free themselves from Russia's advances.

Football is a barometer of life for so many. Football often dictates mood. It can provide hope. Joy. Anguish. It can instil meaning. Focus. Belonging. A purpose.

And football often reflects the lives and communities they serve.

The haves and have nots writ large through stadiums in various states of repair.

Trophy cabinets bursting or barren.

The terrace behind the goal, the cheap seats in the corner, or the plush padded spots at the half-way line – the way you look at football depends on the way you look at life. The way life treats you.

Never more was that apparent than in Moldovan football, where the realities of life have dictated the beautiful game, success and failure, in a profound way.

The oldest existing football club in Moldova is Zimbru Chișinău, who were formed in 1947 as Dinamo Chișinău.

During Soviet rule they were the dominant force in Moldovan football and were the only side from the region to play in the Soviet top tier, playing 11 seasons among the elite between 1956 and 1983. Indeed, in 1956 they finished sixth behind traditional Soviet powerhouses Spartak, Dinamo and CSKA Moscow, as well as Dinamo Kyiv and Torpedo Moscow.

In 1963 they reached the quarter finals of the Soviet Cup, and when not in the Soviet top-flight, they spent much of their endeavours in or around the upper reaches of the second tier. It was no great surprise that when independence came and a Moldovan League was created, it was Dinamo – or rather Zimbru Chișinău who dominated.

Keen to banish all facets of Soviet influence, Zimbru is the Romanian word for the European Bison that had roamed the region for centuries.

Appearing on both the new Moldovan flag and coat of arms, the Zimbru symbolises strength, pride, and a dogged determination to endure, outlast its oppressors. It preceded Soviet rule, Ottoman rule, the Tatars, Mongols, Goths.

And long after they have gone, the Zimbru remain, albeit with a greatly diminished population. Another victim of the occupations – it has, however, survived. Its population rebuilding.

A perfect inspiration for a new country. A new football league. And it's most successful participant.

Zimbru Chișinău won eight of the first nine league titles between 1992 and 2000. Only Constructorul Chișinău broke the monopoly in 1997, though Zimbru did win the Cupa Moldovei that year.

Zimbru represented Moldova in European competition. Playing a first ever continental fixture against Beitar Jerusalem in the qualifying rounds of the Champions League in 1993, they went on to face the likes of PSV Eindhoven, Tottenham Hotspur, Sparta Prague, Shakhtar Donetsk and Hertha Berlin as they attempted to become the first ever Moldovan team to qualify for the group stages.

They didn't make it, and, depending on your world view, no Moldovan team ever has – even though the records show that Moldova *has* been represented at the latter stages of the continent's premier club competition. Sheriff Tiraspol formed in 1997, playing out of the capital of breakaway Transnistria, but within the Moldovan football pyramid. Bankrolled by Sheriff, the second largest company within Transnistria (formed in the early 1990s by two former KGB agents and "operating within nearly all forms of profitable private industries in Transnistria") the club has come to dominate Moldovan football.

Twenty-one league titles since 2001, 12 cup wins, seven super-cup victories, Sheriff Tiraspol has played in the group stages of the Europa League on six occasions, and in 2021 reached the holy ground of the Champions League group stages.

Drawn in the same group as eventual winners Real Madrid, Inter Milan and Shakhtar Donetsk, Sheriff beat Shakhtar two-nil in their opening game, then shocked the world by beating Real Madrid two-one at the Santiago Bernabéu in their second fixture.

Three-one defeats home and away to Inter Milan, and a three-nil loss at home to Real Madrid – with goals from Alaba, Kroos, and Benzema – saw Sheriff end in third place.

But the world had learned the name Sheriff Tiraspol, had heard of Transnistria, but maybe not so much Moldova.

Sheriff, whose owners have significant ties with the politics of Transnistria and with Moscow, have become more a shining light for the breakaway region than for the country they represent on the continental stage. Their dominance, yet another attempt to convince Moldova that a better, more prosperous future exists by looking east, and aligning with Moscow.

Zimbru Chișinău's last silverware – a Moldovan Cup win back in 2014 – compared to the unparalleled success of Sheriff, another avenue of threat to the integrity, the unity of the nation.

But while it may hurt, this lack of success, and the abundant successes coming from Transnistria, it has not swayed Moldova – as witnessed by the EU referendum, the electing of Maia Sandu, a politician wanting closer ties with the west as president before that.

Helping with this – something that Transnistria can only look on enviously at – is the national football team of Moldova (a Transnistrian National Football Team, complete with a crest displaying the Soviet hammer and sickle and a red star were once part of CONIFA, the Confederation of Independent Football Associations, but left in 2017. As an internationally unrecognised state, the Transnistrian National Team are unable to compete in UEFA and FIFA competition, or against national teams from theses bodies. To date, Transnistria have yet to play a competitive match).

Formed a full year before independence, the Moldova National Football Team began a new era with a four-two friendly defeat against Georgia in Chișinău.

While Georgia declared independence from the Soviet Union in April 1991, it wasn't finalised until December of that year. So, the brave new sporting dawn for both fledgling nations in July 1991 happened when Moldova and Georgia were still technically Soviet Socialist Republics.

No matter the geo-political technicalities, change had arrived, and football played a huge part in defining national pride and identity across the newly liberated nations of eastern Europe.

For Moldova, it would be Alexandru Spiridon who would go down in history as the first ever Moldovan to score an international goal for his country (albeit in an unofficial fixture unrecognised by FIFA).

Spiridon would play a central role in Moldovan football in its early years, winning the first ever Moldovan player of the year in 1992, before going on to lift the new Moldovan league title five times with Zimbru Chișinău, and becoming national team assistant coach in 1994 while he was still playing for his country.

But it would be his goal in that first-ever match, replying to an early strike from Georgia's own history-maker Temur Ketsbaia – who would go on to become a cult hero at Newcastle United in the late nineties – that Spiridon is best remembered for.

Moldova and Spiridon's next taste of international football wouldn't come until May 1992, with a one-all draw against another country re-emerging from behind the iron curtain: Lithuania. And it wouldn't be until August 1992 that Moldova would taste victory for the first time at the Jordan International Tournament in Amman.

Moldova would go on to beat Pakistan five-nil and Sudan two-one (with Spiridon scoring his second and final international goal for his country), before one-nil defeats to the hosts Jordan and Iraq. A final fixture, a third-place play-off against Congo saw Moldova come out on top by three goals to one.

The year would be rounded off with a final goalless friendly match in Yerevan against Armenia – another nation taking its first independent steps out from beneath Soviet rule.

An 18-month hiatus would follow while Moldova first joined UEFA in 1993, and then FIFA in 1994. And it would be in September of that year that Moldova would finally play an official, competitive match in world football – a historic one-nil win away to Georgia in the first round of EURO 1996 qualifying fixtures.

Alexandru Spiridon would captain his nation in Tblisi for that landmark occasion in September 1994 and would do so again one month later when Moldova beat Wales three-two to record a first-ever home competitive win. Moldova would only register a third win in the last group game of the qualifiers at home to Georgia (who, despite losing both games to Moldova, finished a creditable third in the group behind Germany and Bulgaria with five wins and five defeats) and would finish fourth on nine points, above Albania and Wales. A solid return from a first stab at a competitive qualifying group, it would herald the beginning of Moldova's international football journey, but the end of its first-ever goal scorer.

Alexandru Spiridon would last until March 1995, when he captained his nation one last time in a three-nil defeat to Albania in Tirana, before moving into coaching full-time.

To date, their EURO 1996 qualifying campaign remains one of their most successful. They did win three matches in the 2012 qualifiers, but two were against a Sammarinese side who conceded 53 goals without answer across their ten fixtures.

Beyond that, Moldova have finished near the foot of every European qualifying group they have taken part in.

They have traditionally struggled even more in World Cup qualifying groups, having won just five of the 68 qualifying fixtures they have taken part in since their first campaign to reach France 1998.

Their best return came in the qualifiers for Brazil 2014, where two of their three wins came against San Marino, two-nil and three-nil, as well as a five-two win away to Montenegro. Beyond that, four of the seven World Cup qualifying groups Moldova have taken part in have resulted in no wins.

In the poorest country in Europe, it is not hard to see why Moldova have struggled while other post-Soviet nations have fared better. Opportunity, infrastructure and development are harder to come by, stability even more so, as witnessed by the fragility of Moldovan club sides.

Dacia Chișinău won the Moldovan Super Lig in 2011 – one of only three sides to break Sheriff Tiraspol's monopoly since 2001. They competed in Europe against Schalke 04 and Hamburger SV. In 2018 they were dissolved.

Sfântul Gheorghe Surunceni were runner's up in the Super Lig in 2019 and collapsed among financial problems and a match-fixing scandal in 2023.

The list of dissolved Moldovan football clubs, and some successful football clubs at that, is extensive and outnumber those in existence today many times over.

It is not easy to be a footballer, or a football lover in Moldova. There are many obstacles in the way of success, and even longevity. And fewer reasons for optimism and hope.

But in the EU referendum and closer economic, legislative, and collaborative ties with Europe, with greater protections against Russian destabilisation, there is one.

And in the Nations League Moldova has another.

Like so many nations ranked near the foot of Europe's footballing ladder, the Nations League has been a catalyst for Moldovan football.

Where World Cup and European qualifying campaigns yielded minimal success, the first three Nations League seasons provided Moldova with a platform to build upon, complete with opportunities for regular morale-boosting results. And with them, a building of pride, belief, and hope among supporters and players.

The 2018 edition saw Moldova finish third in their group behind Belarus, who they played out goalless draws, home and away, and Luxembourg – who inflicted the only chastening defeat of the series with a four-nil defeat in Luxembourg City in their opening match. The return match was far more competitive, ending in a one-all draw in Chișinău.

One-nil and two-nil wins against San Marino rounded out a positive set of matches and saw them promoted to League C for the 2020 season.

In a much tougher group, Moldova struggled against a Slovenian team on the rise (which would culminate in qualification for EURO 2024, where they would reach the round of 16, only being knocked out by Portugal on penalties).

Losing one-nil away, and four-nil at home, this was followed up with two-nil defeats to Greece, home and away. The only point of the 2020 Nations League season (played entirely behind closed doors as a result of the Covid-19 pandemic) came in a one-all draw with Kosovo. A one-nil defeat at the empty Fadil Vokrri Stadium in Pristina finished off an underwhelming, and perhaps unrepresentative season.

Without the boost of supporters, friends and family in the stands, having to get changed in makeshift changing rooms to comply with Covid-19 containment protocols, travelling on socially distanced buses and planes with only a handful of your teammates, it was a very surreal, muted, and sterile environment.

It is hard to know just how the 2020 Nations League may have panned out in less exceptional times, but Moldova's response in 2022 certainly blew away the memories of 2020.

Four Nations League, League D, wins against Andorra, Liechtenstein and Latvia (in that two-one win in Riga from Chapter Four) – promotion was denied purely on goal difference – brought back a sense of momentum, a renewed belief in the national team, that rolled over into qualifying for the 2024 European Championship.

Finishing behind three teams in Albania, Czechia, and Poland, who would all go on to make the finals in Germany, Moldova remained unbeaten at home for the entire qualifying campaign, drawing with Albania, Czechia, and the Faroe Islands.

Better was to come against Poland in June 2023, where an 85th minute winner by Vladislav Baboglo saw Moldova beat a side captained by Barcelona striker Robert Lewandowski (who also got on the scoresheet) three two at Zimbru Stadium, Chișinău.

On their travels Moldova picked up three points in Tórshavn with a one-nil over the Faroe Islands (now regulars in Group C of the Nations League after promotion from Group D) and a draw in front of 51,000 in Warsaw.

An equaliser from Karol Świderski was enough to save Poland from defeat that night – a defeat that would have seen Moldova swap places with Poland to go up into third. As it was, Moldova would remain just a point behind a nation used to qualifying for World Cups and the Euros.

Momentum would continue into 2024 with a one-all friendly draw with North Macedonia and a four-nil victory over the Cayman Islands in March, followed by a three-two win in a friendly against Cyprus in June. The only blot on Moldova's record going into the 2024 Nations League was a four-nil friendly defeat to Euro 2024-bound Ukraine in an emotionally charged fixture on June 11 in Chișinău.

No Ukrainian National Team fixture had been played as close to the Ukrainian border since Russia's invasion began in February 2022. Just 50 kilometres separates Chișinău from Ukraine, and 10,000 spectators crammed themselves inside Zimbru Stadium in a show of unity and defiance, where the result was secondary, but also comprehensive. A rare opportunity to play in front of so many of their countrymen, women, and children, so close to a homeland they are unable to play in, a motivating factor incomprehensible to those of us who have never had to experience the trauma of invasion, war, exile.

Few would have begrudged Ukraine's emphatic send-off to Germany. Few did. The result, unrepresentative of the upward trajectory Moldova had been on since that positive Nations League effort in 2022.

And now, with the 2024 Nations League season about to begin, and a group draw against Malta and Andorra – two sides in and around them in the FIFA World Rankings – another opportunity for progression loomed.

More fixtures to inspire pride and belief. More fixtures to celebrate an identity, a sense of belonging in a cultural enclave largely overlooked, forgotten by the outside world, that has endured nonetheless, surviving and overcoming invasion and oppression since time began, one football match at a time. The next, setting Moldova off on the right footing into this new campaign.

A two-nil win over Malta on September 7 in Chișinău - thanks to goals from Mihail Caimacov and Ion Nicolaescu – was followed up three days later with a one-nil friendly win against a San Marino side still jubilant from their first ever competitive victory.

Meanwhile, in Andorra la Vella, the capital of Andorra, a Ryan Camenzuli goal was enough to give Malta the three points against their hosts in their second Nations League match.

With Moldova due to play Andorra at home next, followed by a trip to Malta, four days in October would do much to determine Moldova's destiny, and a potential first ever topping of an international group. Which would be a significant, definitive milestone. Proof in black and white of progression. All that passion on the pitch and in the stands of the Zimbru Stadium, laid bare, undeniably, for any who cared to look. A landmark to ignite joy and pride.

And with it, promotion back up into League C of the Nations League…

Chișinău on a non descript Thursday lunchtime in October is laid-back, benign. Traffic staggers between one set of traffic lights and the next away from the airport and toward town in a languid, listless flow.

There is no leaning on the horn, no gesticulation at cars switching lanes at the last minute. There is traffic. There are traffic jams. This is life.

Life brought into perspective perhaps by the numerous cars with Ukrainian number plates among them. A little flash of blue and yellow alongside an unfamiliar set of numbers and letters.

There are too many of them to be travellers, tourists. They are a symptom of a bigger ill just 50 kilometres away, where Moldova becomes Ukraine. Problems like these appear more than enough to let a little erratic driving slide. Perspective focused by two years of war on their doorstep.

Life also seems to be happening at three-quarter pace elsewhere. Temperatures in the mid-20s – where t-shirts and shorts could more than suffice – has pedestrians walking at a leisurely tempo here and there.

None are wearing t-shirts and shorts. This is autumn after all, just autumn Moldovan style. After a long hot summer, 23 degrees is nothing to write home about, but it is enough to slow life down to a wander, albeit it a wander with purpose. People still have places to be.

Unlike so many of its Nations League, League D, capital counterparts, Chișinău does not contain a UNESCO World Heritage site. Indeed, it would be fair to say that Chișinău cannot even be described as a tourist destination. Or at least one in the traditional sense.

What it lacks in cultural quarters and old towns with centuries old picture-postcard facades, it more than makes up for with culture of a different kind. And for that Chișinău is as fascinating, captivating as any of the continent's iconic destinations.

Where Chișinău was once a small, regional town, the Chișinău of now, the Chișinău created by the Soviet Socialist Republic, is large and sprawling. Seemingly laid on top of, or around the old town without necessarily obliterating it, the average street is a bewildering assault of contradictions. Tiny, aged homes with shuttered windows and corrugated roofs, little chimneys smoking up into the sky (the type made familiar recently during news reports of rural Ukrainian villages turned into the frontline of the Russian invasion) cower next to huge Soviet Brutalist towers blocks. Little gardens with rows of cane structures to help vegetables grow, swept with the shadow of these vast blocks of concrete balconies and grey windows that don't appear to have been altered since construction 70 years ago.

At first sight Chișinău is stark, maybe even bleak. This sea of tower blocks dominating, whichever way you choose to look, it can be an unsettling, possibly even depressing experience. Not helped by an absence of the familiar.

Chișinău, unlike so many other places across Europe, lacks the plethora of big-name brands adorning shop fronts, restaurant walls and advertising hoardings. The familiar logos that have ingratiated themselves even into World Heritage sites are almost entirely missing here. Moldova has yet to be smothered by fast food outlets, soft drinks logos and fashion brands.

Possibly the tag of Europe's poorest country prejudicing expansion, either way, its absence is at first disorienting, but then, refreshing – this hidden land beyond the mountains. And where the shimmer and neon of these global brands is missing, Moldova has created its own colour.

Where relative poverty, by western European standards, prevents the redevelopment of Soviet-era infrastructure, Moldova and Chișinău find a way.

Vast, beautiful murals adorn the ends of these looming tower blocks, some of which are visibly crumbling, balconies propped up, render fallen away. Flowers, trees, children, rainbows in the colours of the Moldovan flag – blue, yellow, and red – famous figures, anything and everything.

Huge parks are lovingly maintained, complete with boating lakes, forests, kiosks selling coffee and hot dogs, playing music while people meet to play chess and cards outside. Making the most of the mild weather, they are the lungs of the city, and the soul, where groups of teenagers meet to play music and laugh, alongside pensioners eating sandwiches and chatting over the day's events.

Beautiful lakes lined with huge willow trees are glassy, reflecting a scene of tower blocks beyond in softer, pastel shades, diffusing their austerity. Tree-lined pathways wind and loop to little fairground rides, grand flower beds and statues. The city lost completely, but always connected, close at hand, these grand parks inspire modern day Moldova to create beauty and pride through art and ingenuity, and a preservation of what has always made Moldova the country it is – long before the Soviets.

Not far from the grand promenade and stunning steps that flow down into Valea Morilor Park accompanied by cascading water features, the Moldovan academies of Music, Art, and Literature bustle with learning and endeavour.

Elsewhere, the Metropolitan Cathedral of Christ's Nativity is tended to by nuns, some of whom sit lost in prayer beneath a stunningly decorated chandelier, the heady scent of incense, thick, drifting up into the domed spire adorned with a fresco of some heavenly scene.

Away from the busier main street, a smaller church has improvised, with an ornate wooden cross intricately carved with iconography. Two symbols emanating from it weathered over the years, one piece cracked through the middle, it endures, for another little while at least.

And beneath a leafy courtyard, along a residential street, Soviet-era military equipment left behind as the Union collapsed, has been converted into part adventure playground, part museum. An exhibition of the horrors of an old regime, and a warning about the new one amassing beyond Odessa, children clamber across a Soviet jet fighter, its red star peeling and fading on the tail-fin.

Elsewhere, a missile loaded on the back of a launcher, points menacingly at the building across the courtyard, while tanks and armoured cars face in different directions – as if abandoned chaotically and in a hurry. In the warm afternoon, people find seats on piles of decommissioned munitions, absently looking at their phones while their children explore.

On every street Chișinău seems to confound. With little dwellings with chicken-wire fences, brutalist tower blocks, old-abandoned buildings falling down, newer abandoned ones never completed, beautifully coloured monasteries and churches in vibrant blues and yellows. Parks, big or small, the odd dog lazing in the sunshine. And people. Who don't expect to see tourists, or many of them at least.

A woman tending a little museum on Moldovan history is pleasantly surprised at a visitor. A group in traditional dress on top a converted water tower giving a panoramic view of the capital stepping back quickly as I approached.

It is clear that not many people come here. Certainly not enough to generate a need for shops selling local wares to souvenir hunters and the usual tourism trappings.

Chișinău can't compete with the likes of regional capitals Bucharest, Budapest, and Sofia.

It is a completely different kind of place.

And that is neither a good nor a bad thing.

Chișinău is a city, Moldova is a country, not helped by factors it can do nothing to control. Russia's attempts at undermining Moldovan democracy at every step, at preventing closer ties with the EU, NATO, breakaway Transnistria's reputation for being a black-market hub for an illegal arms trade, the war in Ukraine – though stalled – perilously close to the border. All have produced travel warnings by the British Government, and a reputation undeserved.

This little-known or explored region, with a closed currency only available within Moldova's borders, a volatile Russian-backed breakaway region, mere kilometres from the capital, infrastructure from a bygone era buckling under the weight of a modern world – Chișinău, Moldova is so much more than that, if only viewed with an open mind.

The people are warm, community driven, where public spaces are cherished, and the austere beautified. It may not be the Acropolis, the Colosseum, but a pride in who they are, and where they have come from has made Chișinău a living, breathing museum. A testament of survival, of flourishing in the face of seemingly insurmountable, or at least, relentless obstacles.

And as the sun begins to go down on this non-descript Thursday, as clouds of gnats flit on the warm air beneath willow trees, the parks are abuzz with chatter, among other things on the EU referendum that could create countless opportunities for the nation. That could help set it free from Russia's clawing – or set it on a collision course with Putin.

Old friends sit on park benches watching children swish up and back on bicycles. Teenagers listening to music on their phones laugh and mingle in groups beneath the trees. Municipal workers break from their tasks to watch the world go by, joining small groups of men at the kiosks smoking cigarettes, drinking coffee, reading the paper.

There is a buzz of chatter. Not just on the politics of the day, the latest music, local gossip, but on the game. Because in just a few hours the Moldovan national football team are in action…

As the floodlights strengthen and shine up into a sky ablaze in reds and oranges as the sun sets, Zimbru Stadium comes to life.

Built in 2006, it stands beneath a vast Soviet-era 14-storey complex of flats that sweeps around it on two sides like a huge, brutalist harbour wall. Lights begin to flicker across the sea of windows as people make it home from work, dinners are made, while – beneath a canopy of trees in its courtyard – the sounds of children playing.

On the end of the complex closest to the stadium looms one of Chișinău's vast murals. A stunningly beautiful 150-foot-high painting of a young girl in a bobble hat and brightly coloured clothes – one hand holding a bunch of blue flowers – the other stretching up to reach a sea of large orange stars trailing ribbons of colour. It is arresting in its detail, its size, and its quality.

People stop and stare for a moment, pausing beneath it. Lost for a moment as others bustle past them through the turnstiles.

A fine addition to Chișinău's open air art gallery.

Zimbru Stadium seats 10,000, though the small stand on the far side of the pitch, and the block of four rows of seats above the main tier of seating in the main stand remain idle.

And while the official attendance may top out at 6,442, more are watching than that, when the balconies and windows in the tower above begin to fill with bodies.

Silhouettes in windows, parties of people crammed onto balconies, toasting each other's health with the chinking of beer bottles, a Moldovan flag being waved here and there – the people of the apartment complex more than make up for the empty stand beneath them.

A wall of support 150-feet-high few national teams can boast, even in the grandest of stadiums. They settle in as kick off looms.

For those inside the stadium it is a carnival atmosphere. The last home fixture of what has been a positive year for the national team has created a feel-good factor – manifested through excited children carrying enormous bags of popcorn, posing next to cardboard cut-outs of their national team heroes, taking penalties into a mini-goal.

A small stall selling shirts and scarves builds a line of families eager to deck their young ones out in replica tops. Beautifully designed with traditional Moldovan folk patterns woven into the fabric, the countries coat of arms on one breast, the National Team badge on the other, it is part history lesson, part cultural celebration, part sporting iconography.

And at less than half the price of national team shirts from the UK, they are gratefully received by wide-eyed children on tiptoe to see over the stall, pointing at which of the red, blue, or yellow shirts they would like.

Eagerly they pull them over their heads, beaming up at overburdened parents trying to juggle payment with armfuls of hastily discarded tops, popcorn bags, and drinks bottles.

All three shirts – each a section of the tricolour Moldovan flag – seem to take turns as Moldovan home colours. This international cycle it is yellow that seems to be taking centre stage, and as such, yellow is doing a roaring trade, dominating the sea of colour, as the crowds make their way to their seats. Propelled by a sense of hope and that special Nations League ingredient – expectation.

With Moldova ranked 152 in the world in the FIFA standings, and with Malta in 172nd spot (having already been dispatched at Zimbru Stadium two-nil in September), it is the turn of Andorra who should, at 164, statistically give Moldova a sterner test. Though this is clearly not enough to dampen the mood among the Moldovan faithful.

Spread across a network of towns and villages nestled along narrow tracts of valley floor, Andorra is a nation hidden among the spectacular folds of the Pyrenees. The fifth smallest UEFA nation, with only Liechtenstein, San Marino, Gibraltar and the Faroe Islands possessing smaller populations, it sits landlocked on the France-Spain border, virtually equidistant between Toulouse and Barcelona.

Andorra is a relative newcomer to international football, the result of a peculiar quirk of Andorran geo-politics. Despite gaining independence from France in 1814, it didn't form a constitution to become a Republic that could be recognised by the United Nations, UEFA, and FIFA until 1993. For 180 years Andorra simply existed as a place in the mountains. Neither one thing nor the other.

During that time, football in Andorra straddled borders in order to play competitive football.

FC Andorra, the oldest club in the country, was formed in 1942, and competed within the Spanish football pyramid as a de-facto national team for a nation not yet founded.

But when the 1993 Constitutional Referendum created the Andorra recognised today, FC Andorra decided to remain within Spanish football, rising and falling across the Spanish lower leagues, though competing for the most part in the third and fourth tiers.

It remains a proudly Andorran entity within Spanish club football (though its 2024 squad contains just the one Andorran) – but it has relinquished the role of representing Andorran football beyond its relatively newly constituted borders.

The Andorran Football Federation was formed in 1994, a national league created in 1995, with an Andorran National Football Team joining UEFA and FIFA in 1996, losing its inaugural match six-one to Estonia in November – Agusti Pol scoring his country's first ever goal. It would turn out to be the one and only international goal he would score in 28 appearances.

For the next two years Andorra would play a series of friendlies, including an impressive three-nil defeat to Brazil in a World Cup warm-up match that saw Rivaldo and Cafu on the scoresheet.

They picked up a first ever draw in a goalless friendly with Azerbaijan, before setting off on a first-ever qualifying campaign for Euro 2000.

Andorra would lose every game in that qualifying group, which was no great surprise. Maybe what was a surprise was the margin of defeat. Newly crowned World Champions France won two-nil in front of 75,000 in Paris and only one-nil in the return, and Andorra remained competitive in all but one of their other matches (a six-one defeat in Moscow to Russia the only blot on their otherwise respectable debut on the international stage).

It is this competitive edge that has defined Andorra ever since. Rarely winning (their first international victory coming in a 2-0 friendly defeat of Belarus in 2002, a second coming two years later with another two-nil win, this time against Albania), but rarely losing heavily, Andorra have always been a tough nut to crack.

This dogged endeavour was rewarded with a first competitive win in October 2004 over Macedonia (as they were known then) by one goal to nil. Draws away to Macedonia, and home to Finland made that 2006 World Cup qualifying group Andorra's most successful to date.

And while it would take another 13 years for Andorra to record a second competitive win, beating Hungary one-nil in qualifying for World Cup 2018, the fine margins of defeat throughout their international life have seen Andorra remain a tough opponent for even the world's brightest and best.

Since that famous win over Hungary in 2017, Andorra have won three more competitive matches: one-nil in 2019 at home to Moldova during Euro 2020 qualifying, and two-nil and three-nil wins over San Marino during the World Cup 2022 qualifiers.

A decent return for one of the continent's minnows, but respectful defeat remains the by-line for Andorran football.

Another country the Nations League was designed to help. And in their results, a slow and steady progress can be charted.

In the inaugural 2018 season Andorra drew four of their six matches, remaining unbeaten at home against Latvia, Kazakhstan, and Georgia, and picking up another point in Riga.

2020 – as for a number of the minnow nations – saw a little regression in the sterile, behind-closed-doors environment of a Covid-19 world.

A home draw with Malta the sole point secured in a closely-fought group with the Faroe Islands, Malta, and Latvia.

However, 2022 would be something of a breakthrough season, beating Liechtenstein home and away, two-one and two-nil respectively, while going another Nations League group unbeaten at home, with draws against Moldova and Latvia.

The highest points total ever accrued, the most victories in a single campaign, the Nations League in 2022 gave Andorra (like it has all UEFA's minnow nations) an even sturdier, more expressive and expansive base to build from.

But it would be a base they would have to build from without their talisman. Without Andorra's greatest footballing icon.

For 26 years, if anyone were to think about Andorran football at all, it would most likely be Idefons Lima Solà that would spring to mind. A player who, up until late 2023, had been pretty much ever-present in the entire history of the Andorran National Football Team.

Making his debut in Andorra's second international match on 22 June 1997 against Estonia, centre back Lima would also score the first of his 11 international goals across 137 appearances for his country.

He would line up against that Brazilian team in 1998, he would be there for Andorra's first competitive win in 2004. He would be there for the next in 2017 against Hungary. Their third against Moldova in 2019, their fourth and fifth against San Marino in 2021, and their sixth against Liechtenstein in 2022. It would only be the seventh competitive win in the return match against Liechtenstein that Andorra would achieve without their living legend.

Only one of three men to have played international football across four decades (Billy Meredith of Wales and Jari Litmanen of Finland preceded him), Lidefons Lima's last international goal came 24 years after his first when he scored against San Marino in 2021.

In between those two landmarks, he also found the net against Cyprus, the Republic of Ireland, Malta, Azerbaijan, Belarus, Belgium, Wales and Israel.

And when his last international appearance came on 12 September 2023, he became the longest serving player in the history of men's international football.

A true football legend. And one that Andorra were having to come to terms with doing without – this 2024 Nations League season would be the first the national team would have to traverse without him, in its entire history.

True to Andorran form, this new competitive era began in a closely fought game at home to Malta, where only the finest of margins could separate the two. A Ryan Camenzuli goal on the stroke of half time would prove the difference, the first points of the 2024 Nations League would return with the visitors to Malta.

But, in defeat, there were positives, one of which being the burgeoning talent of their young centre forward Albert Rosas. Maybe the next Andorran talisman of a new era.

A season playing in the third tier of Spanish football with Real Betis B, Rosas switched to FC Andorra to be the only Andorran on the roster of a team recently relegated from Spain's second division. A high standard, befitting this upcoming young player.

And with five goals already in an international career spanning just 19 matches, it is Rosas that elicits the largest cheer from the handful of Andorran supporters in the stand above the players tunnel as he jogged off the pitch to prepare for the battle ahead, having just fizzed four or five shots into the roof of the net past Andorra's reserve keeper.

Players and supporters alike steeling themselves for what would most likely be another match of fine margins.

Flags from the huge tower block waved, as they did across the stands as the teams came out for the national anthems – hands across chests, clutching their hearts, as anthems are sung.

Their meaning acute, heavy on the air among a pride in belonging, the Moldovan Limba Noastră – meaning "Our Language" – laden with even more significance and emotion among EU referenda, a war on their doorstep, and aggressive interference from breakaway regions – a primal roar as the last notes drifted up into the night sky, signalled defiance, steadfastness, and the beginning of a passionate support that would endure from first to last.

Behind the goal, in the shadow of the vast tower block complex, an orchestrated group of some 100 – all wearing different versions of Moldova's blue strip used since 1994 – whipped up the support with song and drum.

Watching them, awestruck, a young boy of eight or nine, also wearing a blue strip, with 'Vlad – 8' printed on the back, cannot take his eyes off them.

His father, sat next to him, encouraged him to join in, showing him how to do Moldova's answer to the Icelandic thunderclap, raising his arms above his head, clapping in between the rhythmic, tribal drumbeats. The young boy put down his huge bag of popcorn, watching his dad, the supporters behind the goal. At first his claps were a little off, but then he got it, and by the time the rhythm became fast and furious he was a part of the spectacle, clapping with excitement at its end, looking up at his dad with a broad grin. The next generation beguiled, enchanted, hooked, for life.

When the supporters behind the goal began their repertoire of chants, Vlad joined in with "Hai-Moldova." Too excited to sit in his seat, he kept standing up, his father gently guiding him back down – nodding to those behind who smiled warmly, the young boy's enthusiasm too wonderful to find issue.

In between songs, thunderclaps, awed wonder, the boy (who, in a homage to one of the region's most infamous sons in Vlad The Impaler, or Vlad Dracula – a feared Warlord of the medieval Carpathians, and inspiration for Bram Stoker's timeless character) would come to be known, by me at least, as "Vlad the Inhaler" for devouring a bag of popcorn so big he could barely hold it – finally stared out at the action on the pitch as he ate.

Action that ebbed and flowed.

And while Moldova had the better of the possession, holding onto the ball, passing it around confidently, probing the Andorran backline, when Andorra did get the ball, they managed to cut through Moldova to create good opportunities – denied only by steadfast defending and agile goalkeeping. Albert Rosas at the centre of much of Andorra's attacking threat.

It was a captivating match, played right on the edge – where one slight mistake could be the difference between two even and attack-minded teams.

As it turned out, it wouldn't be a mistake that broke the deadlock, just a period of devastatingly precise passing by Moldova, turning defence into attack in an instant.

A ball out of defence onto the left wing, a surging run, a near perfect cross into an onrushing Artur Ioniță (who, as one of Moldova's most successful footballing exports, had a spread in the match programme celebrating his 10 years playing in the top two divisions in Italy) swept the ball home from the edge of the box into the corner of the goal. A fifth international goal on his 75th international appearance.

Zimbru Stadium erupted. The block of flats behind celebrated with the dancing of phone lights, torches, the waving of flags, while in the stands Vlad the Inhaler hugged his dad, watched the vociferous support behind the goal writhe and leap, congregating back around the drummer for a new round of "Hai-Moldova."

The rest of the half was played out with Moldova on top. The goal pushing them forward for more, the crowd roaring them on. Enthralled, the supporters responded enthusiastically. – another product of the Nations League in providing consistent, concentrated, and winnable fixtures for all. A new way of celebrating their nation, not just in belonging, in the pride of a homeland, but also in the ability of their team. In victory. In regular victories, where heroes are born.

For the teams in League D of the Nations League, these emotions had never been a given before. But now they were, they were coalescing, starting to spill out into other qualifying campaigns. A pride swelling. Nations bolstered. Crowds rapt.

Half time came to save Andorra, who, with the time to reset, came out for the second period with a renewed vigour.

And as time went on, Andorra began to push Moldova further and further back, began to press in on the Moldovan goal. Albert Rosas and his colleagues turning the defence, who had to make more last-ditch tackles, the gloves of Moldovan goalkeeper Dumitru Celeadnic stung by more frequent Andorran strikes on goal.

As the half wound down it seemed almost inevitable that Andorra would score. But Moldova held firm. And as the game crept into added time and Andorra grew more desperate, another piece of incisive Moldovan passing saw them break away from another fearsome rearguard inside their penalty area. Substitute Virgiliu Postolachi driving the ball down the pitch before passing to another substitute, Maxim Cojocaru who, with all of Zimbru Stadium raised to their feet with the breathless passage of play, slammed the ball past Iker Álvarez into the net on 95 minutes.

The roar of delight was visceral, ecstasy displayed through clenched fists raised to the sky, faces following up into the night in some supplication to the footballing gods. Others hugged, some jumped up and down. Some hugged *and* jumped up and down in bundles of jubilant bodies.

And with that goal, right at the death, that rare joy at a football match: absolute certainty that your team is going to win.

Still celebrating, the supporters didn't watch the match restart, didn't watch it finish moments later. Already lost in the pride, the happiness of another win for their national team, the referee's whistle came almost as a disappointment, wanting the moment to last a little longer. No matter. They would celebrate nonetheless.

The support behind the goal carried on with their songs, jumping in unison to the drumbeat. Young Vlad, checking to make sure that he had demolished his entire bag of popcorn, hastily dropped it again to join in with his dad in a final burst of "Hai-Moldova," before a round of applause – celebrating each other, their efforts, as well as the team out on the pitch.

And with that, the stands began to drain away in an excited chatter. Children amassed at the hoardings pitch-side in the hope that they might get a high-five from one of their heroes who were shaking hands, hugging their defeated opponents. Others filed out into the night beneath the mural of the young girl reaching for the stars – an apt motif for such an evening of national pride and achievement.

Slipping away into the streets of Chișinău, a halo of floodlight persisted in the dark skies above, casting a beacon of celebration that could be seen and felt from all points in the capital.

The beautiful mural, the looming tower block complex persisted too. As did the benign, relaxed atmosphere generated by the people that animated Zimbru Stadium.

Walking back through darkened streets engulfed on either side by vast rows of Soviet tower blocks, Chișinău felt as safe, as welcoming as its football supporters. A much maligned, stereotyped, and belittled city revealing its true heart and identity, where pointing and smiling at pictures on a menu overcame language barriers, and were met with an equally strong smile and welcome – even at the end of the night's service. Dinner before bed secured.

It may not have the abundance of traditional old-town tourist destinations. It may be dominated by the austere façade of a bygone regime. It may sit hidden, off the beaten path, visited infrequently when compared to other European capitals. But considering it on these criteria alone does Moldova a disservice and denies potential visitors a unique experience.

Its history and culture exist in a living, working mass of old and new. The streets are its museums and art galleries. The parks its soul, the people its heartbeat. And its football team, the unifying force of a country living on the edge of war, of aggressive destabilising sabotage by Russia.

And like the football team, the country stands firm, voting in favour of joining the EU, voting back in a leader not cowed by Russia, who wants more opportunity for her country, her people.

Progress is fragile, slow. But the momentum is there. With every brave vote, Moldova is pulling further and further away from Russia's grasp and moving toward a new self-determined future.

Progress for the national football team moves on a similar trajectory.

Two wins from two put Moldova on the brink of the League D, Group 2 title. But three days after their win over Andorra at Zimbru Stadium, an 87th minute penalty by Teddy Teuma in Ta' Qali, Malta, saw the hosts take the points, and bring them level with Moldova at the top of the group.

For Malta and Moldova, their fates will be decided by matches against Andorra – Moldova away in the Pyrenees, Malta at home in mid-November.

And it is no given that Andorra will simply yield and give up the points.

Based on two narrow defeats by the finest of margins, who would bet against Andorra winning both games, creating a three-way tie on six points?

It is a group where the benefits of the Nations League are writ large, both statistically in league tables and results, but also on match days in far-flung venues.

Everyone has everything to play for.

Players and supporters dare to dream.

Roll-on November…

Line-ups: 10.10.24, Zimbru Stadium, Chişinău

Moldova

1 Dumitru Celeadnic
2 Oleg Reabciuk
4 Vadislav Baboglo
7 Artur Ioniţă (1) (Maxim Cojocaru (1) 71')
8 Nichita Moţpan (Denis Marandici 57')
10 Vitalie Damaşcan (Virgiliu Postolachi 57')
11 Mihail Caimacov (Victor Stînă 71')
14 Artur Craciun
15 Victor Mudrac
20 Sergiu Plătică
22 Vadim Raţă © (Dmitri Mandrîcenco 82')

Andorra

1 Iker Álvarez
3 Marc Vales © (Marc Pujol 88')
5 Max Llovera
6 Christian Garcia
11 Albert Rosas
15 Moisés San Nicolàs
16 Àlexandre Martínez (Ricard Fernández 61')
17 Joan Cervós
20 Joao Da Silva (Eric Vales 71')
21 Marc García (Aarón Alburquerque 61')
22 Ian Olivera

Nations League D Group Two

07.09.24 – Moldova 2 Malta 0
10.09.24 – Andorra 0 Malta 1
10.10.24 – Moldova 2 Andorra 0
13.10.24 – Malta 1 Moldova 0

	P	W	D	L	F	A	Pts
Moldova	3	2	0	1	4	1	6
Malta	3	2	0	1	2	2	6
Andorra	2	0	0	2	0	3	0

Chapter Nine – Liechtenstein v San Marino
November 18, 2024

DESCRIBING AN ACHIEVEMENT in football as a miracle feels like it is doing a great disservice to the endeavour, hard work, and talent needed to pull it off.

How can a miracle occur, how can an unlikely win be proscribed as such when more than 90 minutes play preceded it?

That is not a miracle, that is a feat of passion, skill, organisation, teamwork, planning, and maybe a little good fortune – overcoming previously-thought, insurmountable odds?

I always believed miracles were the preserve of religious fervour, of statues crying tears of blood:

An event that appears inexplicable by the laws of nature and so is held to be supernatural in origin or an act of God.

I hadn't heard of a second definition of a miracle:

One that excites admiring awe; a wonderful or amazing event, act, person, or thing.

Now *this* miracle, this is the stuff of sporting comebacks and inspired victories. This definition has room for all the effort that is needed for a miracle to occur in football.

No divine act of a benevolent higher power, but the culmination of hours, weeks, months, years of training. Of learning from defeats. Of developing a way of playing that best expresses you, your teammates, the country you represent.

And then, finally, after 20 years – victory. And not just victory, a first-ever competitive victory, after 38 years of trying.

A miracle for Nicko Sensoli, for San Marino.

One miracle born out of another.

San Marino's historic one-nil competitive win over Liechtenstein in September 2024 could only have happened because of the Nations League. Otherwise, the likes of San Marino, Liechtenstein, Andorra, Gibraltar, Malta and Moldova would forever be discarded as bottom seeds in World Cup and European qualifying groups – destined never to meet, other than at the foot of the FIFA rankings for the continent of Europe.

But while preserving their right to feature against the giants of the world game – all 54 nations being treated as equals – the Nations League has enabled a different opportunity.

An opportunity for close-fought matches and attacking intent, scoring goals, winning games, developing ability and confidence on the pitch, and pride and identity off it.

In what it has given nations and their football teams, especially at the foot of the pyramid, the Nations League is the miracle.

A simple, yet revolutionary idea, preserving the sanctity of all nations being equal, while affording opportunity the like of which has never been experienced before in European international football.

San Marino beating Liechtenstein to record only their second-ever win, and their first-ever competitive victory – three points in a league table – is the symptom of a miracle.

The Nations League itself has created the environment for *admiring awe; a wonderful or amazing event, act, person, thing.*

And despite everything the competition had already achieved – San Marino's win was reported all around the world – the Nations League had not quite finished for one campaign.

As it turns out, it wasn't even close…

Leaving the lowlands surrounding Zurich, the scenery begins to quickly ramp up into the picture-postcard notion of what Switzerland looks like. Grand mountain peaks, pasture populated by cows – the soothing chiming of bells from their harness as they wander, vast glassy lakes, steep mountainsides strewn with wooden chalets, complete with peaked roofs to manage the snow, and walls of chopped logs to fend off the cold that will come with it. Neither have quite arrived just yet, with snow only on the mountain tops, the air chill, but not the sharp alpine cold of mid-winter.

If you didn't know it was there you could quite easily miss Liechtenstein entirely, its 61.97 square miles tucked away beneath breathtaking mountain vistas from above, and the Rhine River, complete with a steep, tall berm to fend off any flooding when the winter snow melts below. A main road sweeps along, following the contours of the river on toward the borders with Austria and Germany. Miss the turning into Vaduz and there is every chance you will miss Europe's fourth smallest country altogether.

Landlocked between Switzerland and Austria – the border with the latter straddling high mountain ranges passable only on foot by the most skilled of hikers – this anonymity has served it well throughout history, seeing off empires and dynasties quietly.

Within this anonymity, its people have existed for centuries, tending land and livestock. The Walsers, a mountain community, settled in 1300 in what is now Liechtenstein's highest altitude working town, Triesenberg, (the only part of Liechtenstein clearly visible from above the berm) before the area was formally constituted as an independent country and named the Principality of Liechtenstein in 1719.

Luck too has been on Liechtenstein's side in preserving this quiet peace. During World War II it escaped Nazi occupation when Operation Tannenbaum, the plan to invade Switzerland and Liechtenstein to unite all German-speaking populations into the Reich was shelved.

With that, Liechtenstein has existed, quietly and unassuming behind its natural borders. A population of 40,000 as distinct and defined as any other. Proud of their homeland, their history, and what makes them a Liechtensteiner. Quietly existing beneath the spectacular Alpine mountains around them.

We have already learned that Liechtenstein's love for football resulted in the formation of a national football team in 1981, entering the international football fray in June 1981 in the unlikely setting of the Presidents Cup in South Korea.

We learned that Ludwig Sklarski became the first ever Liechtensteiner to score for his country in a one-all draw against Malta in their first-ever match.

We learned that Donat Marxer scored a hat trick against Indonesia a few days later to become the first player from Liechtenstein to ever achieve the feat, and the first Liechtensteiner to score the winner for his homeland.

We also learned that this achievement has only happened 15 other times in the 43 years since, and only eight times in competitive fixtures.

We discovered that it took until October 1998 for Liechtenstein to notch up three points in a qualifying campaign – Martin Telser scoring the winner in a two-one win over Azerbaijan in a Euro 2000 qualifier – and that, subsequently, competitive international wins would come sporadically, sometimes five or six years apart.

We also discovered that the Nations League has been as much a tonic for Liechtenstein as other League D participants, playing out closely fought, competitive fixtures.

In 2018 they beat Gibraltar two-nil at home and followed that up with a two-all draw against Armenia. In 2020 they beat San Marino away, and picked up draws against Gibraltar and in the return match against San Marino.

In 2022, despite losing all six games against Latvia, Moldova, and Andorra, they were close-fought.

And in 2024, after defeat to San Marino and that excellent comeback in Gibraltar in September, Liechtenstein would break their 40-plus match win-less run with a one-nil friendly victory over Hong Kong, followed by another Nations League draw with Gibraltar in the October International window.

But what we haven't learned about Liechtenstein football so far is the peculiar quirk that exists in Liechtenstein's domestic football scene. A quirk that exists nowhere else: the tale of the Liechtensteiner football clubs with no national football league to play in.

With any law, there is always someone just on the wrong side of it. A victim of circumstance. This time, seven victims – though quite possibly none see themselves as such.

When UEFA and FIFA came up with the arbitrary total of eight teams as a minimum needed to form a national football league, it is unlikely they did so with the intention of excluding anyone.

A national league with eight teams – its winner qualifying for, at the very least, the Champions League preliminary rounds, the national cup winners the Europa League equivalent – it seemed a reasonable stipulation. It is doubtful it was made with the knowledge that only one nation would fail such criteria – Liechtenstein. And, in truth, until 1972, Liechtenstein hadn't even been close to that minimum target.

Club football has existed in Liechtenstein since 1932, when FC Vaduz, FC Balzers, and FC Triesen were founded. They were immediately absorbed into the Swiss football pyramid, and with the exception of three years in the late 1930s where a mini-Liechtenstein football league took place between them (FC Triesen winning the last edition in 1937, remaining to this day the reigning Liechtenstein football league champions) football in Liechtenstein was, and has always been, played within the leagues of another nation.

Liechtenstein's original three were joined by FC Schaan in 1949, FC Ruggell in 1958, USV Eschen/Mauren in 1963, and finally FC Triesenberg in 1972. Like their elder statesmen, they filtered into the Swiss football system, and in the intervening years have found their place within that pyramid.

FC Vaduz are by far the most successful, spending much of its modern history in the second division, though sometimes stepping up into the top-flight – their last tilt at it being in the 2020/21 season.

FC Balzers and USV Eschen/Mauren are currently in the fourth tier, FC Ruggell the sixth, FCs Triesen and Triesenberg the seventh, and FC Schaan the eighth and second to last rung on the Swiss football ladder.

Should an eighth team ever be found, these disparate levels would make a Liechtenstein national league uncompetitive and counterproductive for all involved.

For Liechtenstein's club sides, the die has been cast. Switzerland is the only viable option. And no team from the principality will ever represent their country in the Champions League.

But, at least, Liechtenstein *is* represented in Europe's other club competitions, thanks to a national competition that enables local derbies, bragging rights, and the chance to be crowned champions of Liechtenstein.

The Liechtensteiner Cup is a knock-out competition (bolstered by reserve and sometimes even third teams of the principalities seven sides) that has been running since 1946. And just as any league would be, the Liechtensteiner Cup has been dominated by the countries only professional club team.

Of the 77 editions played out since its inception (it was abandoned during the Covid-19 Pandemic) FC Vaduz have won it 51 times, losing in the final a further 13 times.

In the 21st century Vaduz have claimed 21 of the 22 titles, proudly representing their country in Europe.

And in 2022 they became the first team from Liechtenstein to qualify for the group stages when they beat FC Koper of Slovenia, Konyaspor of Turkey, and Rapid Wien of neighbouring Austria in the qualifying rounds to make Group E of the UEFA Europa Conference League.

FC Vaduz's closest rivals in the Liechtensteiner Cup honours stakes are FC Balzers, who have won the competition 11 times, losing the final on 16 occasions. But their last victory came back in 1997 (where they went on to lose five-one on aggregate to BVSC Budapest in the qualifying rounds of the UEFA Cup Winner's Cup).

FC Triesen have won the cup eight times – including the inaugural tournament back in 1946 (they would go on to win five of the first six). The last Triesen win came in 1975, which is also, to date, the last time they made the final.

USV Eschen/Mauren are the only team to have beaten FC Vaduz this century, winning a penalty shoot-out in 2012 after a two-all draw, one of their five Liechtensteiner Cup wins.

They represented their country in the Europa League the following season, losing to Fimleikafélag Hafnarfjarðar of Iceland three-one on aggregate.

FC Schaan have won the cup three times, the last time in 1994 (where they would go on to play Pirin Blagoevgrad of Belarus in the Cup Winner's Cup, losing one-nil on at home and three-nil away), while FC Ruggell and FC Triesenberg have never won it – Ruggell losing the final seven times, the last occasion being in 2019. Triesenberg have made the final twice, losing five-nil both times to FC Vaduz in 2015 and 2024.

Liechtensteiner Cup matches are eagerly anticipated every season and are the highlight of a campaign – a rare opportunity to test yourself against your national rivals, and sometimes even the big boys in FC Vaduz – they animate both supporter and player alike and are cherished.

And while seventh tier FC Triesenberg have the poorest record in the Liechtensteiner Cup, and therefore in all of Liechtenstein club football, they *are*, however, winning in other, quite spectacular ways.

The only side not based on the valley floor, FC Triesenberg's home ground, the Sportanlage Leitawies, is both a breathtaking achievement of engineering, and a visual marvel.

Like the village it represents, FC Triesenberg perches high above the rest of Liechtenstein after a series of steep, sweeping, dizzying switchbacks between thick alpine forest and seemingly precarious chalets.

Clustered around a few natural plateaus, Triesenberg clings to the sheer mountainside that cuts away beneath them.

FC Triesenberg is no exception, the Sportanlage Leitwies is propped up on huge concrete stilts to create a level playing surface. The effect of which when standing pitch side is a footballing equivalent of an infinity pool. From one touchline you look out across to the other, beyond it nothing but the awe-inspiring Swiss Alps on the far side of the valley. It is beguiling and spectacular and must result in the odd goal or two a season due to visiting players getting lost in the vista, switching off for a moment as they stop following the flight of the ball to wonder at the snow-capped mountains. Misplacing a pass as they seemingly loft the ball out into the valley below.

All of Triesenberg, every mundane, everyday facet of it, is elevated (no pun intended) by the location. People washing up by kitchen windows do so from an infinity kitchen window, looking out at the mountains beyond, the valley far below. The delivery bay for the little store is an infinity delivery bay. The restaurant for Hotel Kulm seemingly teeters out into the abyss. The church steps seemingly lead up into the heavens themselves.

The Walser community that first made Triesenberg home some 700 years earlier did so because they too found the spot inspiring – using ingenuity to overcome its precarious mountainside position. Hanging from the sides of older, more agricultural chalets and outhouses, some strange looking implements – long wooden stakes with three or four sets of slanted arms poking out from them – these are driven into the pastureland and hay bails are built around them, the stakes preventing the crops from tumbling down the mountainside.

Locals wander to the shop, the café for a coffee, the churchyard to pay their respects, the post office to pay a bill, weaving between the few tourists still present in November, lost in the landscape – paused mid-step – staring down into the valley, up at the mountains above, across at the beautiful old chalets. It is not that the view is old, it is just that they have, over time, come to live with it without it dominating their every movement. Something the tourists have not, and who stand, as if frozen to the spot, looking out with wide eyes as the sun sets.

A pallet of pastel colours, like the northern lights, illuminating the sky in pale pinks and reds, then greys as the sun dips behind the mountaintops, draining away to ever-darkening hues of blue, until night falls. The mountains fall into shadow, looming in the darkness above, like some terrible rogue wave. Finally, with a shiver of cold, the tourists are stirred from their reverie and make their way inside for a warm fire.

Staring out the window into the night, not able to let go, tourists find themselves looking out at nothing more than vague shadows, the snaking lights of cars far below heading up toward Germany and Austria, or deeper into Switzerland, and reflections of themselves. Haunted looks of wonder, they sit quietly and look out…

Despite Triesenberg's lofty position among the mountains, it is not the loftiest part of Liechtenstein. Up and away from Triesenberg, up ever narrowing roads that zig-zag across perilous slopes, you find the snowline, snow-dusted firs and chalets, and finally the resort village of Malbun.

You also find an eerie silence, an absence of movement, the entire place still, empty, save for the periodic arrival of an empty bus from Vaduz, that pauses for a short while, then leaves as empty as it arrived, slipping away back down toward the valley floor.

It is as unsettling as it is beautiful, this picture-postcard alpine village of traditional Swiss chalets all shrouded in snow, winding their way up into the ski slopes above Malbun.

Slopes that make it such a popular destination in season that there are four overflow car parks. I park in overflow car park number three, not wanting to have to turn back around if there are no spaces up-ahead.

But my hire-car remains the only car in any of the car parks.

Malbun is empty. Ski season not yet begun, Malbun is deserted. Hotels still shuttered. Ski hire shops dark, cafes, bars, convenience stores closed behind dull windows.

Among the stunning scenery of the snow-covered high-Alps that loom above, the beautiful architecture sprawled beneath, there is such a profound absence of humanity that it almost feels sinister. That no one else is here to share the view seems very odd, askew – and scenes from Stanley Kubrick's *The Shining* start running through your head, looking across at a village of Overlook Hotels…

But, in truth, when you live in the Alps, why visit a village not yet in season, when in just a short while it will be bustling with hiking, skiing, tobogganing activities among deep snow and ski runs, and everything will be open and welcoming?

I am nothing more than a victim of circumstance, and the calendar.

Malbun is not yet open.

But when it does, all four overflow car parks will be overwhelmed with visitors. And the ghosts among the silence will be banished.

Time to head back down the mountain, and the relative bustle of Vaduz.

Like its Sammarinese counterpart, the capital of Liechtenstein does not contain the largest population in the principality. Vaduz has fewer inhabitants than Schaan, a short way further along the valley road.

With less than 6,000 residents, Vaduz, like the rest of Liechtenstein feels unhurried, relaxed: living life within its own parameters. Just off the main road, less than 100 metres from the pedestrianised centre, lies a small farmstead. A field of goats watch the cars go by, staring at the odd passerby forlornly, hoping they will take no notice of the sign asking for people not to feed them – as they are very well looked after and have been getting a little overweight with all the extra titbits handed them.

Around them, tilled fields stand fallow, stretching away towards the berm and the Rhine, ready for the next season's crops.

In the town centre ice-skaters swish and glide around the ice-rink that marks the centre piece of Vaduz's Christmas market. Vaduz old-town with its picturesque houses looks on, beneath Vaduz Castle, home to the nations' royalty, standing on a cliff-top overlooking proceedings.

As the skies begin to darken, it is lit up a warm red by floodlights around its base. And as the light drains from the sky, and darkness swallows the mountain it is perched on, Vaduz Castle floats in the sky, visible from most points along Liechtenstein's valley floor. A beacon corralling the nation beneath it.

As skaters skate, and a game of curling plays out on the far side of the rink, watched on by couples, friends and families drinking mulled wine and hot chocolate, as figures flit in and out of quaint shops selling traditional wooden gifts, and laughter from bars and restaurants spills out as doors are opened and closed – another beacon begins to grow in strength, rising up into the cold night air.

Like anywhere in Vaduz, Rheinpark Stadion is not far away. Nestled beneath the berm by the Rhine River, the stadium doubles up as the national stadium and the home to FC Vaduz.

A small, neat, four-sided stadium seating 6,000, it grows in stature as night falls, its floodlights burning up into the icy skies. Outside, the flags of Liechtenstein, San Marino, UEFA and FIFA flutter on the slight breeze funnelling through the valley cowering beneath the looming shadow of the mountains which seem even more menacing in the darkness – channelling the awe of terrible cresting waves rising high above a helpless fishing boat in an ungodly storm.

The mood outside the stadium is charged too. But in anticipation of what is to come.

For both teams, there is all to play for:: history to be made.

After a win at home to Liechtenstein and a narrow one-nil defeat away in Gibraltar, San Marino began the final round of Nations League matches with a one-all draw in the return match against Gibraltar. This left Gibraltar with six points after a win and three draws in their four matches, San Marino on four points after three games, Liechtenstein on two after three matches.

If Liechtenstein could win, it would put them on five points, securing them second spot and a play-off place to fight for promotion into League C – which would be an unprecedented achievement for any Liechtenstein national team.

If San Marino were to draw, they would claim second and that play-off spot – something the Sammarinese had never done before. But better yet, win and San Marino would finish the group with two competitive victories, seven points, and automatic promotion up into League C.

All three achievements would be huge firsts for a country who had never in their entire history won a competitive match until the first round of the 2024 edition of Nations League matches. Win two in three months, after none in 38 years? For a match between two landlocked micro-states at the foot of the Nations League and the world rankings, it felt like a World Cup final for those who began to congregate around the stadium, draped in Sammarinese and Liechtensteiner flags, scarves, shirts.

It felt like everything; though both camps in the pre-match press conferences tried their best to take the pressure off the players. Attempting to normalise these new expectations. Reduce the burden. Make it seem like just any other game.

Liechtenstein coach Konrad Fűnfstŭck did his best to set out his team's approach, without ramping up the tension:

We want to score one more goal than San Marino, and we approach this task with great joy, because we have more to win than lose.

I hope that it is also the case with the players, that they have more joy than pressure in themselves, to be able to achieve something in this game and thus conclude a great 2024.

Konrad's opposite number, Roberto Cevoli also struck a conciliatory tone in his press conference:

Tomorrow we will take to the field to seek success. We are acquiring this mentality, and we will try to always have it.

The boys have understood that to try to do things well it is essential to start with the right approach to the match; therefore, we will try to win from the first to the last-minute tomorrow.

The captains of the two teams appeared less diplomatic, maybe unable to contain the excitement, the charged sense of longing to achieve something both had no doubt dreamt of since they were young boys. Now on the verge of a success after an international career dominated by defeat, both could not suppress their desire for victory, glory, becoming a national hero, going down in the history books – for all time.

Liechtenstein goalkeeper and captain Benjamin Bŭchel tried to keep a lid on the desire of his team:

It is a final that we're playing – and finals are always something special. You don't have to play big tactics, but simply win, and it's the big goal of every single one in the team to be able to play a promotion for the first time.

San Marino Captain Nicola Nanni, fresh from becoming only the fourth Sammarinese international footballer to score more than one international goal in their careers after his penalty against Gibraltar three days earlier (finally banishing those demons of that opportunity denied him courtesy of VAR against Malta in 2022 – his kick propelled with two years of pent-up frustration into the net) could not hide his, and the teams clamour for a first-ever away win, League title, and promotion for their country. He did not even try:

We want to get the three points. We want to win. And we won't back down.

It was clear that the players, no matter how much their coaching staff tried to downplay the opportunity, the occasion before them, were fully locked into the potential for creating a new sporting chapter for their country. In bringing success, glory, joy where there had been precious little before – just those little Sammarinese fables, moments of magic.

Here they were attempting to cash-in moments, split seconds, for an entire league campaign of success. Not one 90-minute victory, but a victory spanning four games, where at the end they came out on top, or in Liechtenstein's case, second, and that shot at play-off glory.

Both sides were tantalisingly close to something never achieved before in their sporting history. And the players could feel it – a good number of whom, on both sides, were amateurs.

And coming from such a position, coming from such small nations, the gap between player and supporter was negligible. If they weren't playing, they would be supporting. And if they were doing neither, they would be working, shoulder to shoulder with those who populated the stands. Or in this instance, congregated excitedly outside the Rheinpark Stadion.

In such circumstances it surely must be impossible to block out all the excitement, noise, and just concentrate on playing a football match.

Time would tell.

You could tell this game was different. Out of the ordinary.

The stadium car park was littered with camper vans with San Marino number plates, flags dangling from aerials. A small convoy making the seven-hour, 600-kilometre trip up and over the Italian and Swiss Alps to Vaduz.

Where the Brigata Mai Uno Gioia usually travelled in single digits to away matches, there must have been close to 100 – their nation's flag draped over their shoulders, wandering around Vaduz, sitting in bars looking out at the ice skating, and now, as the match drew closer amassing outside the stadium.

And when it was time, they filed inside and began to set up a wall of colour: flags, scarves, banners – the duct tape-ravaged, original Brigata Mai Uno Gioia banner, that had been to so many stadiums across Europe, for so many years, without any joy, taking centre stage.

When the players came out to warm up they roared their encouragement, twirled scarves above their heads, jumped up and down, and began in on their repertoire of songs. Stragglers at the bar and food stall, juggling beers and hot dogs hurried to join in, assimilating into the phalanx of blue and white. Each song, one voice stronger, one voice louder.

They didn't stop after the players had jogged back into the dressing rooms. They didn't stop when both teams stepped out beneath a crescendo of rousing music. They only paused, out of respect, to observe the national anthems, singing along, arms around their neighbour to Inno Nazionale, before roaring back into life as both teams broke from team photos, sprinting out onto the pitch.

The time had come.

And as the referee's whistle went, it felt that the die was cast very early.

One side was coping with the pressure, the desire, the ambition much better than the other. One team began to dominate, while the other seemed to struggle to come to terms with the task facing them. The basics seemed to elude them under the pressure of this bigger picture that was clearly beginning to weigh down on them, affect them in ways that they had hoped would not.

San Marino ran through Liechtenstein's players, ran over them, passing around them at will. Wave after wave of attack was built from the back, then, when the moment was right, they found Filippo Berardi, who in turn found Lorenzo Lazzari on the left wing. From there Lazzari darted past statuesque Liechtenstein defenders to whip the ball into the penalty area for Nicola Nanni and an onrushing Berardi to try and convert.

Shots flew over the bar, past the post, into the arms of Liechtenstein's keeper and captain, Benjamin Bűchel, who would start a move forward for his team, only for the ball to come loose after a few passes, and San Marino would advance again.

It was as far from the start Liechtenstein had made in Serravalle in September as could be. Incisive attacks, assured passing, a sense of confidence in their abilities, all fell away right from the kick-off.

Maybe the psychological scars of that defeat in San Marino hadn't been fully understood, the emotional cracks papered over by two solid draws against Gibraltar, and that much-needed friendly win over Hong Kong.

But lining up against San Marino once more, just two months later, and with such a profound collective collapse in form unfolding right before everyone's eyes, it seemed hard to diagnose it in any other way.

Being the butt of the joke across the world, being the first, and only team to have ever lost to the worst national football team in the world. The first and only to lose to them in a competitive match, it is clear those demons, that burden, that humiliation and embarrassment, it weighed heavily on Liechtenstein's players. Adding lead in their boots. A monkey on their backs. And they played with the weight of the world on their shoulders.

Konrad Fűnfstűck had been right to try and downplay expectations, try and ease the burden on his players, but he clearly hadn't foreseen this. Hadn't foreseen his team being steamrollered by a vibrant, coherent team who made every pass count. Whose every decision was a good one. At a tempo that Liechtenstein simply couldn't live with. Ability unleashed with this new-found confidence and belief.

San Marino had a goal disallowed for offside and were threatening again and again.

And it was as early as the 25th minute that the referee began gesticulating to Bűchel in the Liechtenstein goal to stop time-wasting. Their keeper holding onto the ball as long as he could get away with, in the hope that an extra breather would help his players recover and re-set. An extra moment to try and compose themselves, catch up with the intensity and speed of the game around them. To give themselves a fighting chance.

And in one such moment, toward the end of the first half, they did just that: Bűchel passing out from his goal, another pass into midfield to Aron Sele who, with seemingly no passing options open to him, he drove forward into space – at least he was getting the ball further away from his goal.

But as the Sammarinese midfield chased him down, and their defenders backed off him, Sele found himself pushing deeper and deeper into San Marino territory. And with no other red shirts around him in viable spaces to pass to, he kept going, then unleashed a shot from outside the box that flew into the top right-hand corner of the San Marino goal.

In that instant, when his team desperately needed some divine intervention, 28-year-old Aron Sele, midfielder for Swiss fourth tier side FC Young Fellows Juventus, on his 63rd appearance for his country, scored his first ever international goal.

He had a moment or two on his own, watching the ball slamming into the back of the net, arms raised above his head. A moment or two to savour it, the rest of his team so far behind him. A moment before he was swamped by delirious teammates. Because he had saved them, just before half time. Gave them something to hold onto, build upon, protect. And maybe, just maybe, gave them the confidence boost to banish their demons.

As the half-time whistle went, the Brigata Mai Uno Gioia were no less vociferous in support of their team, who had performed with a style and panache, who had dominated the game with superior ability and skill – another Sammarinese fable created in celebrating a moment in time, if not the outcome of a game. Or, in this instance, half a game. Where San Marino's performance was one moment away from being immaculate.

And as the Brigata filed down to queue for more beer and hot dogs, they remained excitable, expectant, chattering amongst themselves, taking selfies with security guards, police, each other. With more than a little joy in their hearts at what they had seen. And more than a little hope at what they might yet see in the second half.

A half that would, for those expectant, long-suffering San Marino fans who had travelled the continent for years, decades, with so very little joy in return, explode into life after just 90 seconds…

With the crowd barely settled back in for the second half, a defence splitting pass into space, Lorenzo Lazzari anticipating the ball, finding himself so far behind the Liechtenstein defenders it seemed inevitable that an offside flag would come. It did not. His timing had been perfect. As was his nerve as he bore down on goal. One touch, two, then an assured shot past skipper Benjamin Büchel.

One-all.

The Sammarinese substitutes, barely settled on the bench after half time, launched themselves back off it, sprinting onto the pitch to celebrate with Lazzari, lost already beneath a pile of starting teammates.

In the stands it was just as joyous, the enclave of San Marino supporters bouncing around in their rows, some spilling down to the hoardings, pitch-side, arms raised to the skies. Unsure what exactly to do once they had reached the bottom, they ran back up the steps and into the arms of friends and strangers alike. All one in their euphoria – watching San Marino score away was a rare and precious thing. A fable for all-time. A precious jewel among all the years of long, fruitless flights, camper van trips, train journeys across Europe in support of their team.

It would not take long for this precious jewel to be added to in a match, a season of unprecedented Sammarinese achievement.

On 66 minutes another incisive pass into the Liechtenstein box brought about a desperate defensive lunge, missing its mark by just the fraction of a second needed to fell the onrushing Nicola Nanni.

Penalty: San Marino.

Amid the celebrations on the pitch, on the San Marino bench, and in the stands, only one didn't react.

Before he had even dusted himself off, got back to his feet, Nicola Nanni was focusing, lost in that place those brave enough to step up and take a seismic penalty kick go.

While others rushed around him, he went to collect the ball. And with it in his hands, he looked down at it, as if in some silent, unspoken conversation with it. Or maybe with his nerves, his mettle, the child that had dreamt of such a moment, his destiny. Still. While the referee batted away Liechtenstein protestations, herding everyone bar Nanni outside of the penalty area, he only seemed to come back to life when the referee spoke to him, and he placed the ball on the spot.

A few steps back. A glance at the referee. Who blew his whistle. Nanni began his run…

It took a few moments for the team, the substitutes to reach him, and when they did, he was quickly lost beneath the jubilation.

Two-one San Marino. Unchartered territory. Thoroughly deserved unchartered territory.

San Marino had been as dominant as they had in the first half. Only this time they were finding the net. And not for the last time.

Ten minutes later, another well-worked passage of play saw Alessandro Tosi away down the left-wing. Cutting in he looked up, passing the ball into the path of onrushing substitute Alessandro Golinucci, who picked his spot, and slotted home past the outstretched Büchel.

Three-one.

Cue another pitch invasion. More supporters tumbling down the steps in the stand, in some attempt to channel the adrenalin, the euphoria possessing them, propelling them forward, back, leaping up and down, falling into fellow supporters' arms.

More than a few with hands on heads in disbelief.

What is this?

What is happening?

This joy. Is it really happening to me? To us? To San Marino?

In the space of 30 second-half minutes in Vaduz, the world changed for Sammarinese football.

From the moment of Golinucci's goal in the 76th minute, San Marino's first-ever away win was not in any doubt. Given the total domination over their hosts, there felt a sense of inevitability the moment Lorenzo Lazzari equalised.

But a long and bruising international footballing history meant that, no matter how good the performance, nothing could be taken for granted. And wouldn't be, by a team and its supporters who had faced down the best with pride and passion, but never with any joy.

But as the second half played out, the last ten minutes in a state of stunned disbelief from all sides, the Sammarinese firsts began to stack up.

It had been the first time San Marino had ever scored three goals in a game. And in doing so, Lorenzo Lazzari and Alessandro Golinucci became only the fifth and sixth Sammarinese players to score more than one international goal.

With Nicola Nanni becoming the fourth only four days earlier against Gibraltar, San Marino's upturn in international football could be backed up with stark fact. In that select group of players who had scored two goals, it had taken 37 years of national team fixtures to fill the first, second and third spots, but just those four days in November 2024 for the next three.

As well as scoring three goals for the first time, at the final whistle, San Marino had secured their first ever competitive away win (their first ever away win of any kind), had gained their highest ever points total in an international campaign with seven, had won an international group for the first time, and had been promoted as champions to league C of the Nations League.

They had also brought another moment of joy, just two months after their first ever competitive win, for the nation of San Marino and its supporters.

For some it was too much.

Tears streamed down supporters' faces, slumping into seats for a moment to try and comprehend what had happened, before being lifted up once more by the emotion of it all, down to the hoardings at the front of the stand, flags and scarves waving. Watching on, as the players celebrated over on the pitch. But that lasted only for a short while.

Every player that had ever pulled on the San Marino shirt had done so with a pride and a passion, with a desire to represent this nation in the face of overwhelming odds. Had trained long and hard, sacrificing much, to do so. To face the great teams of Europe, no matter the result. Facing down heavy defeat, and the mocking by an unforgiving press, raucous opposition supporters – it was they who could say they had played against the game's greats, in the grand cathedrals of football. It was they who could say that they had played for their country, travelling far and wide to do so.

But they had played in front of a support who loved them no matter what. So long as they played their very best. And never gave anything less than their all. Who worshipped them, even in the face of heavy defeats.

A support who travelled at great cost, who supported without ever any joy, for the love of a country, a group of players, and the team they made.

Support that had helped them through bad results. Had helped sustain them.

And it was that support that the players wanted to celebrate with. More than anything else.

Lining up between the centre circle and the edge of the penalty area, the entire squad held hands, then, as one, ran toward the jubilant support, leaping in the air, punching the air, screaming up into the night as they reached the touchline.

But they didn't stop. They kept running. Into the arms of the fans four or five deep behind the perimeter hoardings. Hugging, quite possibly, friends, maybe family, most definitely regular faces in the stands, undoubtedly people they had never ever met before. They hugged and leapt and roared and cried.

Barriers blurred. Lines erased. A sea of arms and heads and flags and scarves. And shirts, as the players disappeared into the throng.

Undiluted euphoria as the mass began jumping up and down, singing the unthinkable:

'Campione, Campione, Ole, Ole, Ole'.

The reality sinking in: winners of the group. Promotion into League C. Champions.

The Brigata were going to need a new flag.

A new name…

It wasn't only the San Marino supporters who had stayed behind. Much of the home support had too, some slumped in their seats. Others stood by the touchline, lost, staring out into a middle distance of despair, or up into the night sky.

It had been a horrendous evening for Liechtenstein, illuminated only briefly by Aron Sele's wonder strike. The team hadn't performed, hadn't given a decent account of themselves. The occasion, their opponent, had overwhelmed them. Completely.

Gracious in defeat, supporters and players looked on benignly at the celebrations among the Sammarinese, before turning back to look at one another – the more senior players staying behind to apologise, holding their hands up in recognition that, maybe for the first time, the team had let the supporters down. Had been beaten the moment the whistle blew.

It had been a scarring night. Physically and psychologically. It would take some time to recover.

But recover they will, you feel.

Sometimes it takes reaching the lowest ebb to start moving in an upward trajectory.

And, for Liechtenstein, this night represented the lowest moment in their international footballing history. By some distance.

But with it comes opportunity. To reset. To develop and bring in new talent. New ideas. Nurtured, tested, in readiness for the next set of international fixtures, the next Nations League.

It was time to leave. To once more leave those who had earned it to celebrate on together, cheers beginning to fade, drifting up into the mountains and the chill night air as San Marino's manager Roberto Cevoli was raised up by his team, hurled up into the air once, twice, three times in honour of his guiding hand. Him applauding the support, once on the ground again – a new round of songs and chanting erupting.

Jubilation unbound. Not wanting to miss a single second. Wanting to witness everything, feel everything – these most precious and rare moments of Sammarinese joy.

No little fable this.

The Nations League 2024 demands an entire chapter in the annals of San Marino's footballing history.

An entire book.

And while San Marino's achievement made news headlines around the world once more, it quickly faded from the news cycle, replaced with the next story.

But in the tiny country itself, in the people who took part, in the people who looked on from near and far, in the stands or hunkered around television screens, the events of the 2024 Nations League will never be forgotten. Will be passed down to the next generation, will be motivational fuel to inspire and guide those that come next – the story of when San Marino became champions…

Everything changes. Nothing changes. A new story has been written. A new chapter. And with it, justification. That they were right, all along. In the face of disparaging editorials, online mockery, patronising and condescending punditry.

They were right.

Their worth already proven, long before 2024, their Nations League campaign simply solidified that fact. The identity, the pride, the passion of this tiny nation never undimmed. Now shining brighter than ever, thanks to their footballing heroes.

Changing everything. Changing nothing.

San Marino. As it always has been, and always will be.

Forza Titani!

But, mostly, that of the San Marino National Team, is a story of David against Goliath comparisons. It is inevitable since we are talking about amateurs who see themselves as professionals.

So, the concerns related to the result become secondary: the passion, the will to be there at all costs and the pride of defending one's flag in the presence of the great European nations matters much more.

Sometimes it is hard: there is no shortage of defeats in double digits. But the San Marino national team has always looked forward, and it always will.

Pride and passion do not shift with defeats, however painful they may be.

The will and pride of being there, beyond the result, this is what constantly feeds the flame of those who take to the field to defend the honour of the smallest republic in the world.

Line-ups: 18.11.24, Rheinpark Stadion, Vaduz

Liechtenstein

1 Benjamin Büchel ©
3 Max Göppel
4 Lars Traber
5 Martin Marxer (Severin Schlegel 84')
7 Marcel Büchel (Kenny Kindle 71')
8 Aron Sele (1)
9 Ferhat Saglam
10 Sandro Wieser
14 Livio Meier (Liam Kranz 71')
16 Fabio Luque Notaro (Philipp Ospelt 84')
20 Sandro Wolfinger (Emanuel Zünd)

San Marino

1 Eduardo Colombo
4 Filippo Fabri
9 Nicola Nanni © (1) (Nicolas Giacopetti 85')
10 Filippo Berardi (Nicko Sensoli 61')
11 Andrea Contadini (Matteo Vitaioli 85')
12 Alessandro Tosi
14 Tommaso Benvenuti
16 Giacomo Valentini
18 Samuele Zannoni (Alessandro Golinucci (1) 61')
21 Lorenzo Lazzari (1) (Marcello Mularoni 75')
23 Michael Battistini

Nations League D Group One

05.09.24 – San Marino 1 Liechtenstein 0
08.09.24 – Gibraltar 2 Liechtenstein 2
10.10.24 – Gibraltar 1 San Marino 0
13.10.24 – Liechtenstein 0 Gibraltar 0
15.11.24 – San Marino 1 Gibraltar 1
18.11.24 – Liechtenstein 1 San Marino 3

	P	W	D	L	F	A	Pts
San Marino	4	2	1	1	5	3	7
Gibraltar	4	1	3	0	4	3	6
Liechtenstein	4	0	2	2	3	6	2

In Group Two, Moldova secured top spot with a 92nd minute Virgiliu Postolachi winner in Andorra La Vella. Like San Marino, Moldova gained promotion into League C as champions.

Malta's goalless draw with Andorra at Ta' Qali three days later was a dead-rubber, with Andorra already consigned to bottom spot, and Malta in second.

Dead-rubber it may have been, but there was still a celebratory mood, as second spot secured Malta a play-off in March 2026. Promotion could still be achieved if they defeat one of League C's bottom sides, Luxembourg.

Gibraltar, like Malta, will have to wait until 2026 for their promotion play-off against a Latvia side who found life in League C tough after their promotion in 2022.

Aside from a four-one defeat to Armenia, and a three-nil loss to eventual champions North Macedonia, Latvia did remain competitive – losing the return matches two-one and one-nil respectively – as well as beating the Faroe Islands at home one-nil and drawing one-all away in Tórshavn.

The gaps between the leagues are narrowing. The play-offs enabling an extra opportunity for promotion, or another season acclimatising to a higher level.

Small, but profound opportunities and steps forward for some of Europe's minnow nations.

Nations League D Group Two

07.09.24 – Moldova 2 Malta 0
10.09.24 – Andorra 0 Malta 1
10.10.24 – Moldova 2 Andorra 0
13.10.24 – Malta 1 Moldova 0
16.11.24 – Andorra 0 Moldova 1
19.11.24 – Malta 0 Andorra 0

	P	W	D	L	F	A	Pts
Moldova	4	3	0	1	5	1	9
Malta	4	2	1	1	2	2	7
Andorra	4	0	1	3	0	4	1

Chapter Ten – Taking Stock

IT IS OCTOBER 2018, and Tórshavn – capital of the Faroe Islands – has been consumed by a near impenetrable fog. Colourful converted wharf buildings that line the dockside materialise, one by one, out of the cold, clawing shroud. Lights from within, framed by neat, white trim and mantle, illuminate the darkness for a step or two, then – like the rest of the building – dissolve away again to nothing behind you.

With the fog, a dead calm. A breathless silence among the deserted streets. Just the faintest of swells within the harbour lapping at the hulls of moored fishing boats.

From somewhere, every now and then, the sounding of a foghorn. Attempting to guide any stragglers toward shelter beyond the harbour wall – engines barely revving, inching in the dark, with zero visibility, home.

In the stillness, the white-out, footsteps are discombobulating, never knowing where they are coming from, and how far away. A pedestrian looming right in front of you, a nod, a smile, an apology, circumnavigating each other, quickly fading into nothingness once more.

In an unfamiliar town, no matter how small, it is easy to become lost when all landmarks have been erased. Only seeing tiny sections of the whole assembling, then disassembling before you in a weather event – while completely beguiling and supernatural – is so frequent and nuanced on this small archipelago in the middle of the North Atlantic, that the Faroese language has 37 different words describing 37 different kinds of fog condition.

I had found myself in a mjørkakógv (very thick fog), that was threatening to derail the very reason I had come to the Faroes.

Thankfully, finally, just when I thought I would never be able to extricate myself from it, a floodlight came to my rescue. Just like the foghorn down in the harbour, this huge, brutalist structure guiding me and other supporters toward Tórsvøllur Stadium, home of the Faroe Islands National Football Team, and only a second-ever Nations League fixture on the islands.

I had no idea, back then, what a profound effect this trip would have on me, on my future. Three days after that first taste of Nations League football among the spellbinding, supernatural fog, and a three-nil defeat of the hosts by Azerbaijan (who celebrated in the murk with the five Azerbaijani supporters who had made the incredible journey from the shores of the Caspian Sea to this remote outpost in the storm-tossed Atlantic) a second Nations league match against Kosovo took place beneath brilliant blue skies and blustery winds.

Between the two fixtures, a violent storm ravaged the islands that flipped waterfalls tumbling out of the mountains back and up the way they had come, like a businessman's tie blown over their shoulder. Rain lashing horizontally, the winds so strong it seemed like it would never hit the ground.

'A bit windy', the woman behind the bar I had taken refuge in described it as. 'In the Faroes', she went on, 'it is a given that you are going to get wet. It is just up to you how wet you choose to be.'

In the bright sunshine, a young girl in an oversized Kosovo shirt utilised the empty rows in front of her to run up and down with the play, shouting and cheering her team on with joyous abandon. Parents and grandparents, all wearing the shirts of a nation, their nation that had only declared independence ten years earlier, after a prolonged and bloody history through the collapse of Yugoslavia and the wars that followed, looked on, at her, at their team.

Having only been accepted into FIFA in 2014, watching their nation play football was still a new experience. And in the eyes of the little girl, her parents, her grandparents, a nation's future and past played out in swirl of innocence, and the wiping away of tears in acknowledgement of every sacrifice and horror experienced, witnessed first-hand, to get here.

And when Milot Rashica opened the scoring for Kosovo in the ninth minute, every emotion they had ever felt in getting to this point seemed to engulf this small cluster of Kosovan support as the players rushed to celebrate in front of them.

Most importantly of all, the little girl jumping up and down, nearly tripping on the hem of her oversize shirt. Who was too young to have experienced what her elders had. And hopefully never would. The bright new future of Kosovo.

In the 50th minute, René Shaki Joensen equalised for the Faroe Islands, sending the home support into raptures. The Skansin Ultras behind the goal, complete with faces painted in the national colours, shirts and flags, Viking hats and drums, erupted, raising the tempo of their chanting, if that was even possible, driving their team on for a winner.

As it was, the match ended one-all. Everyone could feel satisfied.

Both teams had played with an attacking edge, had expressed themselves, just as had happened between the Faroes and Azerbaijan three days earlier. All looking for the win.

Teams that traditionally set up to defend first and foremost, showing their attacking flair. The Nations League enabling a completely new mindset, that would change the DNA of these smaller teams going forward into World Cup and European Championship qualifying.

A new-found confidence and belief spilling over beyond the confines of the Nations League.

The Faroe Islands winning one, drawing one, losing one of their three home games across a two-month period, an unprecedented set of results and points haul. Their supporters too, getting to express their pride and passion, fuelled even more by the animation of the team and their performances out on the pitch.

It was clear for all to see, or all who chose to look, that toward the bottom of the Nations League, profound changes and advances were being made. Even in that first edition, back in 2018.

For me it was intoxicating, watching teams that were institutionally set up to lose, attacking, expressing themselves, winning. Experiencing supporters celebrate positive results as well as simply their pride in their country, felt a privilege. It was magical. On and off the pitch. Visiting stunning locations, exploring their cultures, histories, and people.

Nation states often dismissed out of hand in international footballing terms as an inconvenience, a distraction, as pointless.

They were pointless no more. Or, at least, as the Nations League campaigns rolled through, more and more nations would start to pick up points, scoring goals and claiming wins along the way.

What the Nations League has provided these teams that exist in the lower reaches of the world rankings has been nothing short of transformational, profound – creating fables for supporters and players to cherish. Moments of sporting celebration forged out of success, not simply in the celebration of identity, belonging, meaning.

Though even the architects of the Nations League themselves maybe couldn't have foreseen just how successful, how meaningful, their project would become, and the results they would produce. Even for the worst team in the world.

To a greater extent left behind in the first three editions of the competition, when other nations began scoring, notching up points, winning matches, it was maybe a step too far, even in the minds of those Nations League founders, for their project to affect the fortunes of San Marino in any significant way as well.

Rooted to the foot of the FIFA World Rankings, no competitive victory in their history, nothing even close. Perennial whipping boys, with a seemingly vanishingly small pool of players to ever turn their fortunes around, victory for San Marino in the Nations League, like in every other international campaign they took part in, would probably be measured in the accumulation of more mini-fables for their folklore.

But those Nations League founders had maybe undersold their idea – the impact of those opportunities to play in closely fought, competitive matches, even if ending in defeat – had undervalued, in the worst international football team in the world, the psychological boost those close-fought fixtures provided.

A tangible sense of improvement. A means of expressing themselves. Of *really* playing. Taking the game to their opponents with attacking flair. Ruing narrow defeats, the finest of margins that could have turned those occasional draws into that unprecedented first-ever competitive victory in the history of their country.

Even in the team that the rest of the world (or nearly the rest of the world, save for a small band of disparate supporters, gathering under the Brigata Mai Uno Gioia banner) had given up on, those base Nations League elements had taken seed. Had begun to germinate among the pride and passion within Sammarinese football, within those players desperate to take to the field in the name of their nation. Combining them with the talent, dedication, unending sacrifice, and pure love of the game that inspired them to want to play for San Marino.

In 2022, those taking notice of San Marino's exploits could possibly have foreseen an upward trajectory, and the hint of a better return in 2024. Their performance at home to Malta, exceptional up to the moment Nicola Nanni's penalty was overturned by VAR. Allesandro D'Addario's last-minute strike in the return fixture, a lick of paint away from a Sammarinese equaliser. Two closely-fought matches where San Marino pressed and passed and played their way into excellent positions, only for football's fine margins to swing away from them, and toward Malta.

Their supporters hoped for better in 2024. But none could have hoped, dared, dream for what actually came to pass. None save possibly Roberto Cevoli and his players, the squad peppered with a new young crop of talent, who had grown up watching their team play out close-fought and expressive, expansive football in the first three Nations League campaigns.

Hope had been joined by belief. Bolstered by those near misses and impressive draws. They were in the business of making history. Being a part of something special. Something remarkable, if you hadn't been there to see the genesis of it, thanks to Elia Benedettini and co.

San Marino's first ever competitive win against Liechtenstein in their 2024 Nations League opener was the final piece of validation the competition deserved. In offering up such fantastic opportunities to the teams often forgotten, seen as also-rans in World Cup and European qualifiers. Written off as inconsequential, an annoyance, a distraction from "proper" football business by the game's elite.

Maybe it was an unforeseen by-product of creating a new competition to eliminate meaningless friendlies that did little for anyone – initiating an abilities driven league system based on FIFA rankings, with promotion and relegation between them – that has seen an uptick in performance among those teams in the lower reaches.

One would hope that as much thought was given to the opportunities it would afford nations at the very bottom of the pile. Whether that was the case or not, in Nicko Sensoli's goal, in San Marino's win, the Nations League recorded its most meaningful result ever – for what it symbolised, and how it had come about.

Without the Nations League it is hard to imagine the environment in which this win was forged ever seeing the light of day. The combination of elements needed to foster such an atmosphere of belief, vanishingly small within a traditional qualifying group.

But here, in the Nations League, San Marino had won. And their belief spurred them on.

A draw against Gibraltar, and that first-ever away win in Vaduz – seven points, the most goals scored in one campaign, group winners, promotion up into League C – opportunity, combined with belief, joy, and passion, knows no bounds. San Marino is the very epitome of that.

Football is for everyone. And everyone can have their day. If hope, talent, and passion can meet dedication, hard work, and a never say die attitude.

Otherwise known as San Marino.

But while all that work across four Nations League campaigns, culminating in 2024's two wins and promotion feels seismic, to those who saw it happen at least, it hasn't changed the dial.

The month after their promotion, the new FIFA World Rankings were published.

San Marino remained 210th, and last.

Forty years of defeat anchoring them still, to the bottom.

Everyone else, all 209 other football nations of the world, are still standing on the shoulders of Titans.

It matters not.

History is instructive, but it does not determine the future. Actions of the present do that.

And, in San Marino, with their heroics in the Nations League, they have created a world in which this tiny nation of some 30,000 people can look forward and know that theirs is a footballing future that will no longer be solely inflicted upon them (little fables excepting).

David had his day.

San Marino have had two in three months.

And given their indomitable spirit, togetherness, and passion, they will have more before too long.

Forged, as always, with an unquenchable amount of joy.

Which is, after all, what football is all about.

Where the UEFA Nations League once had a Sammarinese-sized caveat to its otherwise unqualified success, it can now be celebrated as a universally beneficial competition for all 54 members.

With meaningless friendlies banished, the Nations League now produces a platform to test countries against their peers. A good season seeing them promoted, facing an elevated level of opposition. A poor season seeing them relegated, enabling them to regroup, reset, go again the following campaign, with hope of renewed success.

And in League D, bottom spot also comes with plenty of qualifications, plenty of things to take away and build upon.

Despite Liechtenstein's harrowing experiences against San Marino, two draws against Gibraltar, and that friendly victory over Hong Kong that ended their 40-plus game win-less streak, leaves them with a platform to begin their rebuilding and development of the national team.

Similarly, Andorra, with just the one draw in their final match against Malta, competed with the Maltese and Moldova as equals. Those fine margins determining matches – Andorra's near misses being converted by the opposition when in similar situations.

But, in Albert Rosas, Andorra have the makings of their very own Nicko Sensoli, Nicola Nanni, Alessandro Golinucci – on the verge of breaking through and doing something special in front of goal for his country. The Nations League, the perfect breeding ground for Rosas, Andorra, Liechtenstein, to work, grow, and ultimately do something great.

With the Sammarinese blueprint before them, they now know that truly, anything is possible…

It was not only in the men's UEFA iteration of the Nations league that tiny, great things, were happening.

Anguilla – 14 years without a competitive win, 14 years of thumping defeats in sporadic World Cup qualifying fixtures – found the tonic in regular matches within the CONCACAF Nations League.

Slowly, the national team grew, until, on 4 September 2024 all that hard work came together in a two-nil win over Turks and Caicos Islands – ending the second longest win-less streak in international football.

Anguilla went on to play out two closely fought matches with group winners Belize, losing one-nil in both games, before their Nations League season came to and end with a last-gasp defeat to Turks and Caicos in the return fixture. A 95th minute penalty by Ledson Jerome denying them another point, but not denying them second place in the table.

Gigantic strides forward for a team that had been getting soundly beaten, even by those around them in the world rankings only a few years earlier. Another Nations League success story, highlighting what can be achieved, if given the opportunity.

And it is these stories, these opportunities, replicated in the UEFA Women's Nations League – where teams routinely beaten by the world's best in World Cup and European qualifiers, are building through close-fought fixtures in this newer competition – that have inspired two nations to take the leap. That massive next step, into competitive international football.

Both national women's teams of Liechtenstein and Gibraltar announced in late Summer 2024 that they would, for the very first time, compete in a competitive UEFA competition, in the shape of the 2025 Women's Nations League.

A vital stepping stone between friendly fixtures and the daunting prospect of taking on the likes of Spain or Germany in World Cup qualifiers, Liechtenstein's women will first take on Armenia, Kazakhstan, and Luxembourg across three international windows in 2025.

Meanwhile, Gibraltar will face Slovakia, Moldova, and the Faroe Islands.

Tangible, manageable fixtures where confidence can be created, pride, talent, and determination can be built upon, while assimilating into the international football scene.

The Nations League enabling two young teams to take their first steps with excitement and expectation.

When it comes to active, competitive women's national teams within UEFA it is now 54, minus one.

And the one is coming.

In October 2024, on a nondescript pitch in front of precious few, Elisa Terenzi picked up the ball in midfield and drove toward the

Romanian goal. Jinking one way, then the other, she picked her spot, her moment, and chipped the ball over the defence, the keeper, into the top left-hand corner of the goal. The keeper had no chance. Not from the moment Elisa had picked up the ball, had decided what she was going to do.

Just-rewards for a performance in which she had already struck the crossbar for San Marino Women's under-16 side in their six-one defeat to Romania's under-16's.

Progress is slow, but impressive in this young side. And this progress will not be rushed. Young Elisa and her teammates won't be thrown into the cut and thrust of senior women's international football until they are ready. But that time is getting ever nearer.

A team is forming, bonding, coalescing around the talent of Elisa and her friends.

And when the time is right. When they are ready, they will enter the fray – the 54th and final member of the UEFA women's footballing community.

When they do, it will be Nations League that offers them that first, all-important opportunity, and a chance at creating their own mini-fables for their country.

Mini-fables, and who knows what else?

Who knows how Elisa and her friends will take the opportunity afforded them when it comes?

But inspired by the San Marino class of 2024, showcasing what can be achieved with joy and belief, beneath the nurturing wing of the Nations League, when that chance comes, who would be foolish enough to bet against her?

Against her country?

For Elisa, her teammates, they are standing on the shoulders of Titans…

www.ingramcontent.com/pod-product-compliance
Lightning Source LLC
Chambersburg PA
CBHW052033070526
44584CB00016B/2018